Famous Men Throughout History

Trivia On Men Who Made History From Ancient Civilizations To The 21st Century

Compiled by

Cheryl Pryor

Arlington & Amelia

Copyright © 2018 Cheryl Pryor

Arlington & Amelia Publishing

ArlingtonAmeliaPub@cfl.rr.com

All rights reserved. No portion of this book may be reproduced or transmitted in any form or by any means, electronic or mechanical, including photocopy, recording, or any information storage and retrieval system without permission of the author.

ISBN-10: 1886541426
ISBN-13: 978-1886541429

IN MEMORY OF MY FATHER

TABLE OF CONTENTS

About This Book

1	Ancient Civilizations	1
2	Men of the Bible	14
3	Royals & Rulers	19
4	Kings of England: Medieval, Renaissance & The Enlightenment Eras	23
5	Influential Men of European History	31
6	Asian Civilizations	38
7	Incan & Aztec Civilizations	44
8	Explorers	46
9	Pirates & Privateers	54
10	Native American Indians	59
11	Early American History	65
12	Founding Fathers & Signers of the Declaration of Independence	90
13	Civil War	100
14	The Wild West	108
15	Bad Guys: Gangsters, Presidents Assassins, Serial Killers, & Terrorist	113
16	Men Of Science	121
17	Inventors	129

18	Artists	140
19	Authors & Poets	153
20	Musicians	170
21	Athletes	191
22	Men Of War	206
23	Political Leaders & Heads Of State	221
24	Presidents of the United States	233
25	Most Brutal Dictators In History	242
26	Achievements Throughout History	247
27	Men In Modern American History	255

About This Book

'Famous Men Throughout History' is a trivia book with historical clues to aid you in answering the questions. There are questions of all levels from quite difficult to elementary level. Of course the further you go back in history and in foreign lands and leaders the more difficult the questions are. But don't despair, even the tough ones have some interesting facts to learn. The questions get easier as you reach American history and names and events that may be more familiar to you.

Included in the book are over 780 trivia questions with multiple choice answers. Included are over 740 men who have made history – *the good guys and the bad.*

The book begins with Ancient Civilizations and continues through all the eras of history right up to Modern American History.

You will find included men of royalty from kings who ruled the land, pharaohs, presidents, heads of state, and dictators.

Men who ruled the high seas as pirates, notorious gangsters, and men of great accomplishments with science and medicine, along with men who made great discoveries you can test your knowledge on.

See how much you know about the Founding Fathers of our nation, the men who risked their necks by signing the Declaration of Independence, those who fought in wars to ensure our freedom, and presidents.

Test your knowledge on the men from the Wild West who were mountaineers, outlaws, cowboys, or helped forge trails and bring others out to settle the west.

The arts which includes artists, musicians, and writers along with fascinating stories of their lives are all included.

The answers are found at the end of each chapter. The page number of the answer key can be found given at the beginning of each chapter. This way you can test yourself without the answer being visible while you are pondering the answer.

You will find included in the answer section a highlighted area titled **Did you know** that brings the history of these men alive with fascinating tidbits of information.

Some of the men you may recognize immediately, while you may find some you've never heard of that are equally fascinating.

There are a wide assortment of categories with men whose names have become well-known over the ages. Test your memory and your knowledge and see how many of them you know.

*If you find this book interesting be sure to
also look for
'Women In History Trivia.'*

Other Books by Cheryl Pryor

Women In History Trivia

Where In The U.S. Am I?

Where In The World Am I?

The Big Book of Old Testament Bible Trivia

The Big Book of New Testament Bible Trivia

Living The Word of God

The Big Book of Presidential Trivia

The Big Book of First Ladies Trivia

Presidents, First Ladies, & First Family Trivia

Presidents Trivia Challenge

First Family Trivia

Children Of The Presidents

American Revolution & The Birth of A Nation Trivia

Chosen

Pregnancy Journal

Precious Moments

Treasured Moments of My Child

My Mother's Life Story

My Father's Life Story

How Much Do You *Really* Know About The Love Of Your Life?

Couples Game Night Challenge

RV Travel & Expense Journal

Wedding Survival Guide

Write Now

Legacy

Children's Books

My Child's Keepsake Journal

Trivia For Kids: The Presidents

Trivia For Kids: First Ladies

From the series: The Sullivan Family Series

Savannah In The Big Move

Savannah On Stage

Savannah On Horseback

Savannah in Look What Followed Me Home

Savannah & The Grumpy Neighbor

Savannah & The Mad Scientist

From the series: Savannah's World Travels Series

Savannah's Disney World Celebration

Savannah Goes To Paris

1

ANCIENT CIVILIZATIONS

Answers for this chapter on page 10

Ancient Mesopotamian Empire

1. He was the 6th king of the First Babylonian Dynasty and best-known for his surviving set of laws that were once considered the oldest laws put into effect in human history.

    A. Sargon the Great   B. Hammurabi

    C. Naram-sin   D. Tilgath-pilsear

2. This king of Assyria who figures prominently in the Old Testament made Nineveh his capital, built a new palace, and extended the city erecting inner and outer city walls that still stand today.

    A. Sennacherib   B. Ashur-uballit

    C. Sargon II   D. Gilgamesh

3. Which Ancient Mesopotamian king called himself 'King of Kish'?

    A. Shilmaneser V   B. Ashur-uballit

    C. Sennacherib   D. Sargon

4. This ruler of Ancient Assyrian Empire ruled from 745 to 727 B.C., in which time he established the world's first professional standing army. He greatly expanded the Assyrian Empire.

    A. Tiglath-pileser III   B. Sennacherib

    C. Sargon   D. Hammurabi

Ancient Persian Empire

5. In 480 B.C., what Persian ruler invaded Greece, captured Athens, and burned the Acropolis?

    A. Cyrus II   B. Cambyses II

    C. Xerxes   D. Zoriaster

6. In the year 519 B.C. while reigning over the Persian Empire he authorized the Jews to rebuild the Temple of Jerusalem in accordance with an earlier decree by Cyrus.

    A. Herodotus   B. Artaxerxes III

    C. Cyrus II   D. Darius

7. In 525 B.C., he conquered Egypt and successfully overthrew the Egyptian pharaoh during the Battle of Pelusium. His victory brought an end to Egyptians ruling Egypt which held until the 20th century.

    A. Alexander the Great   B. Cambyses II

    C. Xerxes   D. Zoriaster

8. The Persian Empire was founded around 550 B.C. by who?

    A. Herodotus   B. Darius III

C. Artaxerxes II   D. Cyrus II

9. A Greek historian born in the Persian Empire who is referred to as "The Father of History." Who is he?

    A. Herodotus   B. Cambyses II

    C. Cyrus II   D. Darius III

Ancient Asian Empire

10. He was Emperor of Japan during major changes in Japan. It was during his reign that the nation went from an isolationist feudal state to a capitalist imperial world power.

    A. Zhu Di   B. Meiji the Great

    C. Confucius   D. Jalal-ud

11. The Imperial House of Japan, also referred to as the Imperial Family or a dynasty coming from what family, the oldest continuous hereditary monarchy in the world?

    A. Akihito   B. Jimmu

    C. Yakamoto   D. Suzuki

12. Tall and believed to have had red hair and green eyes yet sporting an Oriental look, he was the founder of the Mongol Empire. The empire he ruled became the largest contiguous empire in history – from the Pacific Ocean to eastern Europe.

    A. Genghis Khan   B. Tammerlane

    C. Kublai Khan   D. Jahan

13. He was the grandson of Genghis Khan. He conquered China and founded and became the first emperor of the Yuan Dynasty.

    A. Tammerlane   B. Meiji

    C. Jahan   D. Kublai Khan

14. In the 14th century, this Turko-Mongol military leader conquered most of the Muslim world, central Asia, and part of India. His empire rivaled that in size and power of the domain of Genghis Khan a century earlier.

    A. Atilla the Hun   B. Tamerlane

    C. Akbar the Great   D. Akbar the Great

15. Emperor of Mughal India in the mid-1500's, he was known for his religious tolerance of other's beliefs and for his enduring relations with other empires. For more than four centuries he has been looked upon as one of the greatest rulers in human history.

    A. Jalal-ud   B. Zhu Di

    C. Shah Jahan   D. Akbar the Great

16. This Mughal Emperor ruled from early to mid 1600's. Known for his love of architecture, during his reign India became the richest center of the arts and architecture. While best known for building the Taj Mahal as a mausoleum for his beloved empress, he also built the Peacock Throne, and the Pearl Mosque.

    A. Shah Jahan   B. Jalal-ud

    C. Siddhartha   D. Meiji the Great

Ancient Egyptian Pharaohs

17. Around the year 3100 B.C. he is said to have founded the 1st Dynasty and unified the Lower & Upper Egypt.

    A. Ramses II   B. Menes

    C. Khufu   D. Tutankhamun

18. What pharaoh of the 4th Dynasty built the Great Pyramid (around 2589 B.C. to 2566 B.C.)?

    A. Amenhotep III   B. Djoser

    C. Ramses II   D. Khufu (also known as Cheops)

19. In the book of Exodus of the Bible, the greatest salvation event in the Old Testament, which pharaoh was it that Moses approached beseeching him to let the sons of Israel depart out of Egypt?

    A. Amenhotep II   B. Ramses II

    C. Thutmose III   D. Khufu

20. Which pharaoh ruled from 1479 B.C. to 1425 B.C., and created Egypt's wealth? He was brilliant in battle and is known as the 'Napoleon of Ancient Egypt.'

    A. Menes   B. Thutmose III

    C. Akhenaten   D. Djoser

21. When this pharaoh began his reign in 1390 B.C., Egypt was the richest and most powerful nation on earth. Instead of battling his enemies he tried diplomacy by carving the Amarna letters and sending them to foreign rulers. The letters were a success and kept peace with

other nations.

    A. Tutankhamun   B. Akhenaten

    C. Amenhotep III   D. Khufu

22. What pharaoh of the 19th Dynasty of Egypt is regarded as the greatest and most powerful pharaoh, famous for his exploits during the Battle of Kadush, making Egypt prosperous? He is also known for having built the Abu Simbel.

    A. Ramses II   B. Menes

    C. Khufu   D. Djoser

23. Known as the "Boy King" he was an Egyptian pharaoh in the times known as the New Kingdom. He became a ruler at the age of 9 and was dead before he reached the age of 20. He was virtually unknown until his tomb was discovered by Howard Carter in 1922, going from obscurity to the most well-known pharaoh in history. The discovery of his tomb and the treasures inside was the most significant archaeological find of all time.

    A. Ramses II   B. Khufu

    C. Menes   D. Tutankhamun

Ancient Greek & Roman Empire

24. He was a classical Greek philosopher who was one of the most famous and respected philosophers of all time. He, along with Socrates and Aristotle, laid the fundamentals of Western philosophy.

    A. Homer   B. Pericles

    C. Plato   D. Hippocrates

25. He is viewed by many as the 'Founding Father of Western Philosophy.'

    A. Socrates   B. Plato

    C. Euclid   D. Trajan

26. He is the most well-known of the three ancient Greek tragedians whose plays have survived and influenced the likes of William Shakespeare. His masterpiece was 'Oedipus the King' written in 425 B.C.

    A. Homer   B. Sophocles

    C. Thucycdides   D. Pythagoras

27. He was one of Rome's greatest orators and was one of the leading political figures of the era of Julius Caesar, Pompey, Marc Antony, and Octavian.

    A. Aristotle   B. Leonidas

    C. Erasthenes   D. Cicero

28. He was the founder of the world's first great library and the first to classify plants and animals.

    A. Aristotle   B. Archimedes

    C. Thucycdides   D. Sophocles

29. He is known as the 'Father of Medicine.'

    A. Erasthenes   B. Homer

    C. Hippocrates   D. Claudius

30. He is the most famous mathematician and inventor of ancient Greece who is known for a device for raising water, which is still used in some areas today.

    A. Plutarch   B. Archimedes

    C. Pythagoras   D. Pericles

31. He was one of the greatest ancient historians. His 'History of the Peloponnesian War,' recounts the 5th century B.C. war between Sparta and Athens where he relied on eyewitness accounts and his experiences as a general during the war.

    A. Thucycdides   B. Julius Caesar

    C. Trajan   D. Pericles

32. King of Sparta from about 490 B.C. to 480 B.C., he is known for his leadership in the Battle of Thermopylae, a battle where only 300 Spartans led by the king battled ten times the number of Persian warriors. At the time of the battle the king was 60 years of age.

    A. Hadrian   B. Spartacus

    C. Augustus Caesar   D. Leonidas

33. He is one of the most renowned figures of Ancient Rome and one of the greatest military commanders in history. He became the most powerful man in the Roman Republic with the title of dictator in perpetuity. He greatly expanded Rome's geographic reach and established it's imperial system. He was assassinated on the Ides of March on the steps of the Senate.

    A. Tiberius Gracchus   B. Julius Caesar

    C. Crassus   D. Brutus

34. Heir to the throne, he became the first emperor of the Roman Empire after the death of Julius Caesar. He was one of the most successful Roman emperors, his reign lasted for 45 years.

    A. *Augustus Caesar / Octavian*   B. *Alexander the Great*

    C. *Nero*   D. *Constantine*

35. He became King of Macedonia who overthrew the Persian Empire, and in 332 B.C. the people of Egypt crowned him with the double crown of the pharaohs.

    A. *Claudius*   B. *Gaius Marcus*

    C. *Alexander the Great*   D. *Marc Antony*

Answers - Chapter 1 – Ancient Civilizations

1. B – Hammurabi

Did You Know: *These code of laws are known as the Code of Hammurabi, which were used to regulate Mesopotamian society. The most common of those laws were, "Eye for an eye, tooth for a tooth." There are 282 laws in all and are one of the earliest and most complete written legal codes from ancient times.*

2. A – Sennacherib

3. D – Sargon

Did You Know: *He became the first person in history to create an empire that ruled over a multi-ethnic people. His empire has been described as the first true empire in world history. Legend says he ruled the whole world, but it was actually from the Mediterranean to the Persian Gulf.*

4. A – Tiglath-pileser III

5. C – Xerxes

Did You Know: *This is the same Persian king who married Esther, the first Jewish queen and heroine of the Biblical book of Esther. The book of Esther in the Bible tells of her marrying King Ahasuerus. Many Bible commentaries observe that Ahaserus is the Hebrew version of Xerxes who ruled from 486 to 465 B.C.*

6. D – Darius

7. B – Cambyses II

8. D – Cyrus II (the Great)

Did You Know: *He was ruler of Persia's Achamenid Dynasty and was the writer of the first Declaration of Human Rights. The Declaration of Human Rights has been stated as being the first charter of human rights, predating the Magna Carta by nearly two millennium (predated by 1700 years). In 1971, the United Nations published a* translation in every official U.N. language. It is one of the most precious historical records of the world.

9. A – Herodotus

10. B – Emperor Meiji the Great

11. C – Yamato

12. A – Genghis Khan

Did You Know: His birth name was Temujan but he changed it to Genghis Khan when he became ruler in 1206. Khan's Empire included a large part of China, Korea, Pakistan, Iran, Iraq, Turkey, Afghanistan, Moldova, Kazakhstan, Armenia, Georgia, Turkmenistan, Kuwait, Kyrgyzstan, Tajikistan, Uzbekistan, and parts of Russia. It is believed his armies may have slaughtered more people than Stalin and Hitler combined, an estimated 40 million were killed by his army.

13. D – Kublai Khan

14. B – Tamerlane, also known as Timur the Lame

Did You Know: His tomb, inscribed with the words "When I rise from the dead, the world shall tremble" was excavated in 1941. The excavation revealed he had Mongoloid features, was tall for the time, and he had a debilitating hip injury and was missing two fingers – old battle wounds from his mid-twenties which gave him the nickname, 'Timur the Lame.' Even though his empire rivaled that in size and power of the domain of Genghis Khan, it is estimated that his armies killed 17 million people, about 5% of the world's population at the time, he was unable to become a Mongol Emperor since he was not a direct descendant of Genghis Khan; nor could he claim legitimacy in the Muslim world as he wasn't a descendant of Muhammad.

15. D – Akbar the Great

16. A – Shah Jahan

Did You Know: The Peacock Throne was a jeweled throne, the seat of the Mughal emperors – one of the most splendid thrones ever built. It was ascended by silver steps, the throne sat on golden feet represented by two open peacock tails which were inset with diamonds, rubies, and other precious stones. The throne was taken as a war trophy in 1739 and has been lost ever since.

17. B - Menes

18. D - Khufu (also known as Cheops)

Did You Know: The Great Pyramid took 20 years to build and remained the tallest man-made structure in the entire world for nearly 4,000 years. The base of the Great Pyramid covers over 13 acres with a height of over 480 feet. Sealed in a pit at the base of the Great Pyramid was found an Abydos boat, the most elaborate funerary boat that had been sealed in the pit since circa 2500 B.C. When found the ship was fully intact. It measured 143 feet in length and 20 feet wide. If placed in a body of water today it would sail. It's intended purpose was to carry Khufu to the Sun God Ra.

19. A – Amenhotep II

Did You Know: Many believed it to be Ramses II, but evidence doesn't point that way. The Old Testament never mentions the name of the pharaoh most likely because the book of Exodus is not meant to highlight the pharaoh, but the power of God.

20. B – Thutmose III

21. C – Amenhotep III

22. A – Ramses II

Did You Know: He was one of the longest (2nd) reigning pharaohs. He had over 200 wives and concubines and over 100 children. He was about 90 years at the time of his death. His was the last of Egypt's imperial power. During his reign he became famous for his exploits during the Battle of Kadesh, a military campaign fought against the Hittite Empire to recover the lost provinces in the north. It was the earliest well-recorded battle in history, which occurred in 1275 B.C. and believed to be the largest chariot battle with 5,000 – 6,000 chariots involved. He is also noted for signing the first known international peace treaty – the earliest international peace treaty known to historians.

23. D - Tutankhamun

24. C – Plato

Did You Know: *He founded a university which is believed to be the world's first university.*

25. A – Socrates

26. B – Sophocles

27. D – Cicero

28. A – Aristotle

29. C – Hippocrates

Did You Know: *He developed the Oath of Medical Ethics for physicians. which is taken by physicians even today, known as the Hippocratic Oath.*

30. B – Archimedes

31. A – Thucycdides

32. D – Leonidas

33. B – Julius Caesar

34. A – Augustus Caesar (also known as Octavian)

35. C – Alexander the Great

Did You Know: *It is said Alexander the Great is the one who overcame the Gordian Knot. The legend of the Gordian Knot came from the city of Gordium, modern day Turkey, where upon entering the city was an ancient wagon with it's yoke tied with knots so intricately knotted together it was impossible to see how they were tied together. Much as the sword in the stone legend, it was said whoever could unravel the knots was destined to become ruler of all Asia. Alexander the Great coming upon this immediately set upon unraveling the knot. After a time, unable to unravel the knot he said, "It makes no difference how they are loosed," drew his sword and sliced the knot in a single stroke.*

2

MEN OF THE BIBLE

Answers for this chapter on page 18

1. He was the first man, he was created by God, and is considered the father of all mankind.

    A. Adam   B. Abraham

    C. Noah   D. Joseph

2. God saw how humankind had turned wicked and determined to wipe them from the face of the earth – with the exception of one man who he found to be righteous. He told him to build an ark for him, his family, and two of all living creatures both male and female, and seven pairs of all clean animals, along with food for his family and the animals. Who is this man who was saved from the flood by obeying God?

    A. Job   B. David

    C. Noah   D. Moses

3. He was the founding father of the Jewish nation of Israel.

    A. Adam   B. Saul

    C. David   D. Abraham

4. His wife was turned into a pillar of salt when she disobeyed and looked back at Sodom.

    A. Lot   *B. David*

    C. Samuel   *D. Esau*

5. He was born a Hebrew, was raised by the pharaoh's daughter, and led the Hebrew people out of Egypt.

    A. Aaron   *B. Moses*

    C. Jacob   *D. Joshua*

6. While still a youth he killed Goliath, who not only was a giant but a seasoned warrior?

    A. Cain   *B. Abel*

    C. David   *D. Saul*

7. What man of the Old Testament is known for the virtue of patience?

    A. Judah   *B. Samson*

    C. Samuel   *D. Job*

8. A carpenter by trade and a righteous man, he was Jesus' earthly father.

    A. Joseph   *B. Zacharias*

    C. John   *D. Paul*

9. He is the Son of God, our Lord and Savior.

A. John the Baptist   B. James

C. Jesus Christ   D. James

10. He wore a garment of camel's hair with a leather belt, ate locusts and wild honey, baptized those who repented of their sins in the Jordan River, was a humble man who preached the coming of the Messiah and baptized Jesus.

A. Herod   B. Tiberius

C. Moses   D. John the Baptist

11. Which apostle, previous to following Jesus, was a tax gatherer?

A. Mark   B. Matthew

C. Andrew   D. Thomas

12. He was the apostle that denied Jesus three times as had been foretold to him by Jesus.

A. Peter   B. James

C. John   D. Andrew

13. At the cross, which apostle did Jesus entrust with the care of His mother?

A. Simon Peter   B. Andrew

C. John   D. James

14. Which apostle refused to believe Jesus had risen from the dead until he saw for himself the imprint of the nails from his crucifixion and put

his fingers in the place of the nails and in His side where he had been pierced by a sword?

    A. Peter   *B. Thomas*

    C. John   *D. James*

15. Which apostle's name will go down in infamy as the one who betrayed Jesus?

    A. Thomas   *B. Peter*

    C. James   *D. Judas*

Answers - Chapter 2 - Men Of The Bible

1. A – Adam

2. C – Noah

3. D – Abraham

4. A – Lot

5. B – Moses

6. C – David

7. D – Job

8. A – Joseph

9. C – Jesus Christ

10. D – John the Baptist

11. B – Matthew

12. A – Peter

13. C – John

14. B – Thomas

15. D – Judas

3

ROYALS & RULERS

Answers for this chapter on page 22

1. The duchy of Normandy was founded by this Viking leader in the early 10th century who became the first ruler of Normandy.

    A. Charles III   B. Rollo the Walker

    C. William Longsword   D. William the Conqueror

2. Which king of France was known as the Sun King, one of the most powerful monarchs in French history?

    A. Louis XIV   B. Napoleon Bonaparte

    C. Clovis I   D. Charles VI

3. He was the first Holy Roman Emperor, King of the Franks, and King of the Lombards. He was a medieval emperor who conquered most of western Europe by the end of his reign. He is one of the most well-known names in history.

    A. Otto I   B. Louis I the Pious

    C. Leopold I   D. Charlemagne

4. The Ottoman Empire reached it's fullest extent under his rule. He was Sultan of the Ottoman Empire from 1520 – 1566.

    A. Suleiman I   B. Murad I

    C. Ahmed II   D. Mustafa I

5. He seized political power in France after the French Revolution and crowned himself as emperor.

    A. Louis-Philippe I   B. Napoleon

    C. Charles X   D. Napoleon III

6. He was leader of the Hunnic Empire from 434 – 453 A.D. He's considered one of the greatest barbarian rulers in history with a near perfect record in his battles. He was the last and most powerful king of the Huns reigning over what was at that time Europe's largest empire. His empire stretched from Central Europe to the Black Sea and from the Danube River to the Baltic.

    A. Dengizich   B. Aetius

    C. Ellak   D. Atilla the Hun

7. He was the tsar of Russia who was later proclaimed emperor, founder of the city St. Petersburg, and was grandson to the founder of the Romanov dynasty. He was the first Russian monarch to receive an education in Russia and abroad. He traveled incognito across Europe to form a strong alliance with European nations and was considered one of the country's greatest reformers.

    A. Ivan the Terrible   B. Ivan V

    C. Peter the Great   D. Nicholas II

8. He was the Roman Emperor from the years 161 – 180. He was the last

successor of rulers known as the Five Good Emperors. He symbolized the Golden Age of the Roman Empire and was one of the most respected emperors in Roman history.

  A. Marcus Aurelius   *B. Augustus*

  C. Tiberius   *D. Caligula*

9. King of Prussia from 1740 – 1786, he greatly enlarged Prussia's territories and made Prussia the foremost military power in Europe.

  A. Wilhelm II   *B. William II*

  C. Frederick II   *D. Louis Ferdinand*

10. He was the 5th Roman Emperor and was infamous for his debaucheries. He killed his mother and persecuted Christians. Legend has it that he "fiddled while Rome burned."

  A. Titus   *B. Nero*

  C. Claudius   *D. Caligula*

Answers - Chapter 3 - Royals & Rulers

1. B - Rollo the Walker

2. A - Louis XIV

3. D - Charlemagne

4. A - Suleiman I (the Magnificent)

5. B - Napoleon

Did You Know: *Before he was emperor of France while a military leader and on a campaign in Egypt the Rosetta Stone was discovered. The Rosetta Stone was the artifact that cracked the code of Egyptian hieroglyphics, which was a written language that had been dead for almost 2,000 years. The stone was discovered in 1799 and it wasn't until 1822 – 1824 before the hieroglyphic code was cracked.*

6. D - Atilla the Hun

7. C - Peter the Great

8. A - Marcus Aurelius

9. C - Frederick II

10. B - Nero

4

Kings of England: Medieval, Renaissance & The Enlightenment Eras

Answers for this chapter on page 29

1. One of the most famous literary figures of all time he is from the era of Camelot, a legendary figure with his knights of the Round Table, his sword Excalibur, and his queen Guinevere. So, what do you think...is he a legend or was he real?

    A. Lancelot   B. King Arthur

    C. Alfred the Great   D. Aethelwulf

2. He is the most famous of the Normans. He invaded England and conquered the Anglo-Saxons. He became the first Norman King of England reigning from 1066 – 1087.

    A. William the Conqueror   B. Canute

    C. Stephen   D. Galahad

3. He was King of England for only two years. He is most remembered for being accused of imprisoning his two young nephews in the Tower of London and then having them murdered to protect the throne.

    A. Edward the Confessor   B. Richard III

    C. Edward V   D. Henry VI

4. He is the only English monarch known as "the Great." He was king of the Anglo Saxons who reigned from 871 – 899. He was four years of age when Pope Leo IV anointed him as king. He safeguarded his kingdom against the Vikings.

    A. Aethelwulf   B. Alfred

    C. Edward the Confessor   D. Harold II

5. He was one of the most popular kings in English history. He had a reputation of being courageous, hence his nickname. He raised a substantial fleet and army and took part in the Crusades.

    A. John Lackland   B. Charles I

    C. Stephen   D. Richard I

6. He was the youngest of William the Conqueror's sons, who while King of England, he strengthened the crown's executive power.

    A. Henry I   B. Harold II

    C. William II   D. Richard I

7. This king was the first to be deposed since the Conquest. He was king from 1307 – 1327, at which time he was replaced by his son. He was considered a flawed jewel in the English crown It was during his reign Robert the Bruce set out to regain the kingdom of Scotland.

A. Henry III   B. Edward II

C. Edward III   D. Richard II

8. In the year 865 – 871 this King of Wessex led the conflict against the Vikings.

A. Aethelwulf   B. Alfred the Great

C. Edmund   D. Aethelred

9. Fourteen years of age when his father was forced to abdicate the throne, he became King of England and reigned for 50 years. His reign saw the beginning of the Hundred Years War against France.

A. Henry IV   B. Edward III

C. Richard II   D. Richard III

10. King of England from 1199 – 1216, he was the youngest son of Henry II and Eleanor of Aquitane. Before a king, while his brother, King of England, had left to fight in the Crusades and was imprisoned in Germany he tried to seize control of England, but was unsuccessful. Initially after his brother's release, he was banished but was later recognized as his brother's heir. Facing baronial rebellion he was forced to accept the Magna Carta in the year 1215.

A. Henry VIII   B. James I

C. John Lackland   D. Edward

11. He succeeded to the throne at the age of thirteen, and reigned for only two months, the shortest-lived monarch in English history (unless you take into consideration Lady Jane Grey, the "Nine Days Queen" or de facto queen). He and his brother Richard were murdered in the Tower of London – it is said on the orders of his uncle, Richard Duke of Gloucester, who then had himself named as the rightful heir to the

throne.

    A. Richard III   B. Edward V

    C. Henry VIII   D. Richard II

12. Not only King of England he also held the titles Duke of Normandy, Count of Anjou, and Duke of Aquitaine. He was the first Plantagenet king. He married Eleanor of Aquitaine and through the marriage added much of the area he would rule: most of Wales, Normandy, Anjou, Gascony, and other areas of France. He ruled England from 1154 – 1189. He was father to two of England's more memorable kings: Richard the Lionheart and John Lackland.

    A. Henry II   B. George VI

    C. George III   D. James I

13. He was one of the most recognized kings in English history. He led two successful invasions of France and eventually secured control of the French throne. He was the first king of England since the Norman invasion whose first language was English. He made England one of the strongest kingdoms in Europe.

    A. Stephen   B. William II (Rufus)

    C. Edward IV   D. Henry V

14. He became king before he turned a year old when his father died. He was designated the German king in 1169 and Holy Roman Emperor. He became the most powerful monarch in Mediterranean Europe.

    A. Richard II   B. Henry VI

    C. Edward V   D. George III

15. This king is often considered the greatest of the Plantagenets. He

earned the name the "English Justinian" and was also known as "Longshanks." He had an ambitious plan to conquer the whole of Britain – he conquered Wales, but he was unsuccessful with Scotland. It was during his reign that the Stone of Destiny, a venerated relic of Scotland was taken and incorporated into a coronation chair at Westminster Abbey. During his reign the banner of Scottish resistance was taken up by William Wallace (of the movie 'Braveheart' fame).

    A. Edward I   B. Henry III

    C. Henry VII   D. James I

16. He became heir to the British throne after the death of Queen Elizabeth I as she had no children of her own.

    A. Canute   B. William I

    C. Richard III   D. James I

17. This British king is the most well-known in large part due to his many wives and how he disposed of them when he was eager to marry another.

    A. George I   B. William III

    C. Henry VIII   D. Charles II

18. He was the most popular Prince of Wales Britain ever had. What was more important than being the King of England that would make him abdicate the throne? An American woman named Wallis Simpson who was twice divorced.

    A. Edward VIII   B. George VI

    C. George III   D. William III

19. He was King of England during the Revolutionary War in the

American colonies.

    A. William III   B. George III

    C. James II   D. James I

20. He was known as the *"Merry Monarch,"* and while he was very popular he was a weak king. The Great Fire of London in 1666 took place during his reign.

    A. Charles II   B. Charles I

    C. Edward VI   D. Henry VII

Answers - Chapter 4 – Kings of England: Medieval, Renaissance & The Enlightenment Eras

1. B – King Arthur

2. A – William the Conqueror

3. B – Richard III

4. A – Alfred (the Great)

5. D – Richard I (the Lionheart)

Did You Know: *In the ten years he was King of England he only spent a few months in England and it's doubtful he even spoke the English language. As with many English rulers of the Plantagenet line he was essentially French and that was where his true interests were.*

6. A – Henry I

7. B – Edward II

Did You Know: *Even though he had four children with his queen he was a homosexual. His lover was held captive as the barons rose in rebellion. His queen, known as She-Wolf, gathered support and invaded England and captured the king who was then forced to abdicate. This is the king and queen that were portrayed in the movie 'Braveheart,' though not portrayed with complete historical accuracy.*

8. D – Aethelred

9. B – Edward III

10. C – John Lackland

11. B – Edward V

12. A – Henry II

13. D – Henry V

14. B – Henry VI

15. A – Edward I

Did You Know: *The Stone of Destiny was originally used during the crowning of Scottish kings. Scottish kings were enthroned on the Stone of Destiny at Scone Palace. The legend of the stone dates back to Biblical times and is said to be the same stone Jacob used as a pillow. According to Jewish legend, it became the pedestal of the ark in the temple. The story beyond the legend is the Stone of Destiny remained at Scone Palace until it was "stolen" or forcibly removed by King Edward I. He had it sent to Westminster Abbey and then became a part of the Coronation chair and used on the coronations from King Edward II and every subsequent king and queen of England, including Queen Elizabeth II. In 1950, the stone was stolen by Scottish nationalists who returned it to Scotland. A few months later it was brought back to Westminster Abbey until the year 1996 when it was returned to Scotland and installed at Edinburgh Castle. Upon it's return 10,000 Scottish people lined up along Edinburgh's Royal Mile to witness the historic event of the return of the Stone of Destiny to it's rightful place. After 700 years the stone still remains a powerful symbol of Scottish independence.*

16. D – James I

Did You Know: *He was the son of Queen Elizabeth's main rival to the throne, Mary Queen of Scots who the queen initially kept imprisoned and then had beheaded. He was King James I of England and James VI King of Scotland. He executed Sir Walter Raleigh for treason. He was the first of the Stuarts to sit on the throne of England. He is considered to be one of the most intellectual to sit on the English and the Scottish throne.*

17. C – Henry VIII

Did You Know: *Of his six marriages, two ended in annulment, two in natural deaths, and two were beheaded. Each of his three children were at one time English monarchs.*

18. A – Edward VIII

19. B – George III

20. A – Charles II

5

Influential Men Of European History

Answers for this chapter on page 35

1. He is known as the 'Father of Communism' as his ideas gave rise to revolutions toppling governments that had existed for centuries. He influenced rulers such as Lenin and Mao Zedong. His influence is still felt today and he has been described as one of the most influential figures in history.

    A. Vladimir Lenin   B. C.S. Lewis

    C. Karl Marx   D. Friedrich Engels

2. In 1798 he was the first of the family dynasty to go into the banking business. A prominent Jewish family originally from Germany they established banking and finance houses in Europe beginning in the 18th century – they remain the most famous and infamous banking family in the world.

    A. George Soros   B. Nathan Mayer Rothschild

    C. J.P. Morgan   D. John D. Rockefeller

3. He was a French engineer who designed and oversaw the construction of the most famous site in Paris, which is named after him.

    A. Henri Louvre   B. Robert de Sorbon

    C. Georges Pompidou   D. Gustave Eiffel

4. He was an Englishman whose scientific theory of evolution became the foundation of modern evolutionary studies.

    A. Isaac Newton   B. Albert Einstein

    C. Charles Darwin   D. Karl Marx

5. He was one of the most influential figures of the French Revolution and one of the principal architects of the Reign of Terror.

    A. Louis XVI   B. Maximilien de Robespierre

    C. Napoleon Bonaparte   D. Voltaire

6. This German industrialist and businessman became a hero during WWII when he saved the lives of 1,100 Jews in Poland and Czechoslovakia from certain death at the hands of the Nazis by employing them in his factories which kept them out of the concentration camps.

    A. Oskar Schindler   B. Raoul Wallenberg

    C. Amon Leopold Göth   D. Nicholas Winton

7. In July of 1944 an officer of the German army, a member of the Bavarian noble family, was chief conspirator who plotted and failed in an attempt to assassinate Adolf Hitler.

A. Friedrich Fromm   B. Heinrich Himmler

C. Claus von Stauffenberg   D. Erwin Rommel

8. In 1875 this French sculptor was commissioned to design a sculpture to commemorate the centennial of the American Declaration of Independence.

A. Richard Morris Hunt   B. Frederic-Auguste Bartholdi

C. Gutzon Borglum   D. Gustave Eiffel

9. A German mechanical engineer who in 1885 designed and built the world's first practical automobile powered by an internal-combustion engine.

A. Karl Benz   B. Gottlieb Daimler

C. Wilhelm Maybach   D. Nikolaus Otto

10. He was an English scholar who in 1525 translated the Bible into English and a leading figure in the Protestant Reformation.

A. Martin Luther   B. John Calvin

C. John Wycliffe   D. William Tyndale

11. He was the Holy Roman Emperor from 1765 to 1790. For a time he co-ruled with his mother, Maria Theresa the archduchess of Austria and Queen of Hungary & Bohemia, and then he became sole ruler of the Austrian Habsburgh dominions. He was the brother of the French Queen Maria Antoinette, He is one of the best examples of Europe's enlightened despots.

A. Joseph II   B. Rupert

C. Leopold I   D. Maximilian I

12. He was a military general and became the first emperor of France. He conquered most of Europe in the early 19th century.

    A. Adolf Hitler   B. Marechal de Lattre de Tassigny

    C. Napoleon Bonaparte   D. Charles de Gaulle

13. An English military leader who led parliamentary forces in the English Civil War. After leading the overthrow of the British monarchy he ruled England, Scotland, and Ireland as Lord Protector. He became one of the most famous figures in English history and remains one of the country's most controversial public figures.

    A. Thomas Fairfax   B. John Locke

    C. Charles I   D. Oliver Cromwell

14. He was a German thermal engineer who invented the internal-combustion engine which was named after him.

    A. James Watt   B. Rudolf Diesel

    C. Robert Fulton   D. Gottlieb Daimler

15. He was the most brilliant of the Medici family. During the 15th century he was a statesman and patron of the arts in Florence, Italy – which he initially ruled with his brother Giuliano. After his brother was assassinated he became sole ruler from 1478 to 1492. He was one of the great patrons of the Renaissance with both Bertoldo & Michelangelo as part of his household.

    A. Cosimo de Medici   B. Lorenzo de Medici

    C. Gastone de Medici   D. Piero di Cosimo de' Medici

Answers - Chapter 5 – Influential Men Of European History

1. C – Karl Marx

2. B – Nathan Mayer Rothschild

Did You Know: Nathan Mayer Rothschild came to Britain in 1798 to establish himself as a banker. It was in the 1760's that the Rothschild empire actually began with Mayer Amschel Rothschild. He started out as a rare coin dealer going on to founding a banking business in the German duchy of Hesse. With his five sons the family business spread throughout Europe where their tentacles are still firmly entrenched today where they work secretly behind closed doors with their influence felt worldwide. Their interests and influence goes way beyond banking. They have in the past and continue to obtain influential positions in their respective countries and work towards their hidden agendas. They have been the masterminds behind many major events since the 18th century and continue to use their influence in shaping matters of the world. As early as 1790, Mayer Amschel is quoted as saying: "Let me issue and control a nation's money and I care not who writes the laws." Rothschild is the perfect example of a family dynasty that elevated themselves through deception and other unscrupulous means. Rothschilds have influenced the world around us as well as the world within us for centuries. From the founder of the Rothschild family to the ones in our present day, all claim to be of Jewish ancestry — a claim that has been instrumental in their elevation as the most powerful family in the world, and yet they are accused of anti-Semitism and not without good reason. The family is known to and encouraged to intermarry first and second cousins to "keep it all in the family." The family's estimated net worth is considerably more than $350 billion. Their properties around the world make the queen's home at Buckingham Palace look minuscule.

Did You Know: Karl Marx's grandmother was a first cousin of Nathan Mayer Rothschild's wife.

3. D – Gustave Eiffel

4. C – Charles Darwin

5. B – Maximilien de Robespierre

6. A – Oskar Schindler

Did You Know: While Oskar Schindler was a member of the Nazi Party, he did save 1,100 Jews saving generations of Jewish families. Initially it was done with ulterior motives in mind, such as profit. But that doesn't take away from the lives he saved.

How many of you have heard of Nicholas Winton? Winton is called the "British Schindler." A friend had asked this London stockbroker to come to Prague to help at a refugee camp. While there he realized the Nazi's occupation of the country was inevitable. He organized the rescue of 669 children, most of them Jewish, from Czechoslovakia during the Second World War in an operation later known as the Czech Kindertransport. Winton found homes for the children and arranged for their safe passage to Britain. The last trainload of children left on August 2, 1939, bringing the total of rescued children to 669. On September 1, 1939 the biggest transport of children was to take place, but on that day Hitler invaded Poland and the borders were closed putting an end to the Czech Kindertransport. Winton remained haunted for the rest of his life of the fate of the children left behind. After the war he never told a soul how he had saved hundreds of children – not even his wife. It was half a century later when his wife found a scrapbook in the attic with pictures of the children along with their names and information that she first learned of the heroic acts of her husband. His wife shared the story with a Holocaust historian and the newspapers. Children he had saved began to write letters to him and to come to express their thanks for his saving their lives. The rescued children, many then grandparents, referred to themselves as Winton's children. He passed away in 2015 at the age of 106 blessed with a long life. Up to the time of his death he wore a ring given to him by some of the children whose lives he saved. It is inscribed with a line from the Talmud, the book of Jewish law. It reads: "Save one life, save the world."

7. C – Claus von Stauffenberg

Did You Know: Even though he was a member of the German army, he was horrified by the actions of Adolf Hitler and the Nazi Party. Operation Valkyrie, a mission planned by von Stauffenberg and other anti-Nazi Germans, was a plot to assassinate Hitler and overthrow the Nazi Party. Having access to Hitler, von Stauffenberg himself would set the plot in motion. Armed with explosives in his briefcase he armed one of the explosives and placed it beneath the table where Hitler sat. The bomb detonated killing four but only injuring Hitler. Von Stauffenberg was executed by firing squad, his pregnant wife, and other family members were questioned and sent to concentration camps and his children, under Hitler's orders, their names were changed and they were given to be raised by an SS officer's family. His wife and children were later liberated.

8. B – Frederic-Auguste Bartholdi

9. A – Karl Benz

10. D – William Tyndale

11. A – Joseph II

12. C – Napoleon Bonaparte

Did You Know: *There are a few things you may not know about Napoleon.* ***1)*** *It was Napoleon's army in Egypt who discovered the Rosetta Stone – the artifact that provided the key to cracking the code of Egyptian hieroglyphics.* ***2)*** *He once wrote a romance novel.* ***3)*** *Beethoven originally planned to dedicate his Third Symphony to Napoleon. The title of the symphony is 'Bonaparte,' and when published in 1806 the title page read, "Sinfonia Eroica…composed to celebrate the memory of a great man." Beethoven's attitude toward Bonaparte did a complete turnaround when he discovered Bonaparte had declared himself Emperor. He scribbled out the title of the symphony so violently that it tore the page.* ***4)*** *Napoleon attempted suicide before his exile in Elba. Forced to abdicate after his disastrous campaign in Russia he was sentenced to live out his life in exile. Napoleon attempted suicide by taking a poison pill he carried with him. Over time the pill had lost it's potency and while it did make him violently ill, he was still very much alive.*

13. D – Oliver Cromwell

14. B – Rudolf Diesel

15. B – Lorenzo de Medici

Did You Know: *In the year 1478 in an incident called the Pazzi Conspiracy a group including the Archbishop of Pisa, with the blessing of Pope Sixtus IV, the group attacked Lorenzo and his brother and co-ruler Guiliano in the Cathedral of Santa Maria del Fiore in an attempt to seize control of the Florentine government. Guiliano was brutally stabbed to death, but Lorenzo was able to escape with only a minor wound. In the aftermath of the Pazzi Conspiracy, the Medici and Florence suffered from the wrath of the Holy See (the papacy and those associated with the pope). They then seized all the Medici assets, excommunicated Lorenzo and the entire government of Florence. The pope was not punished in any way for his involvement of the murder and attempted murder, all due to greed and power.*

6

Asian Civilizations

Answers for this chapter on page 42

1. He was the Mongolian warrior and ruler who created the largest empire in the world.

    A. Xiahou Dun   B. Kublai Khan

    C. Genghis Khan   D. Lu Bu

2. He lived in the 6th century B.C. and is best known of all Chinese philosophers.

    A. Laozi   B. Confucius

    C. Han Fei   D. Mencius

3. For many years the Xia Dynasty of China (2070 – 1600 B.C.) was considered more mythological than based in reality. All that changed in the 1960's and '70's when sites were discovered that put that theory to the test. Who was believed to be the founder of the Xia Dynasty?

    A. Jie of Xia   B. Qi of Xia

    C. Emperor Shun   D. Yu the Great

4. In 1949, with the promise that everyone would be equal the Cultural Revolution movement was led by what leader?

   A. Lin Biao   B. Mao Tse Tung

   C. Chiang Kai-shek   D. Zhou Enlai

5. The Warring States period (between the 5th and 3rd centuries BC.) are the three centuries when rival Chinese states battled for dominance. The Qin state would ultimately win the battle. It is then that this man, King of Qin, unified the other states under his rule and proclaimed himself as the first emperor of China.

   A. Ying Zheng (Qin Shi Huang)   B. Li Si

   C. Lü Buwei   D. Lao Ai

6. He was a political and military leader who served as the leader of the Republic of China between 1928 – 1975, first in Mainland China until 1949 and then in exile in Taiwan.

   A. Sun Yat-sen   B. Chen Jiongming

   C. Chiang Kai-shek   D. Lin Sen

7. The grandson of Genghis Khan was known for conquering China and becoming the first emperor of the country's Yuan Dynasty.

   A. Timur   B. Kublai Khan

   C. Zhenjin   D. Tolui

8. In 1839 which emperor tired of British drug smuggling so he had British warehouses seized confiscating chests of opium destroying them which brought on the First Opium War?

   A. Daoguang   B. Xianfeng Emperor, I-ju

C. Puyi   D. Yixin, s Prince Kung

9. He was the last Emperor of China and puppet emperor of the Japanese controlled state of Manchukuo.

    A. Guangxu   B. Feng Yuxiang

    C. Qin Shihuang   D. Puyi

10. Samurais were warriors in the noble class during feudal Japan. They worked under daimyos, large landowners who they served to protect. Name this samurai whose name is one of the most recognizable in Japanese history noted for his cunning and strength. In a battle where he was outnumbered 8 to 1 his foe was killed and this famous samurai was the victor, the most unlikely victor in Japanese history.

    A. Atilla the Hun   B. Toyotomi Hideyoshi

    C. Oda Nobunaga   D. Shah Jahan

11. After the year 838 B.C., Japan became an isolationist country with continuing only a very minimal trade with China. Which shogun changed this policy opening the doors to Japan and allowing trade with the outside world when Commodore Perry arrived in 1853-54, ending the 220 years of national seclusion?

    A. Tokugawa Ieyasu   B. Emperor Meiji

    C. Chairman Mao   D. Dalai Lama

12. Japan produced the world's first novel, 'Tale of Genji,' written by this man circa 1020 B.C.

    A. Confucius   B. Murasaki Shikibu

    C. Katsuhiro Otomo   D. Mishima Yukio

13. He is the current leader of North Korea (as of the year 2018).

    A. Kim Jong-un   B. Kim Il-sung

    C. Kim Jong-il   D. Kim Il

14. From the 9th to the 15th centuries the Khmer kingdom at Angkor was the most powerful and architecturally prodigious culture in Southeast Asia. Today the most memorable site is Angkor Wat, a temple complex in Cambodia and the largest religious monument in the world. Construction took place around 1113 – 1150 A.D. on over 500 acres. What king is credited with the building of Angkor Wat?

    A. Norodom Sihamoni   B. Jayavarman II

    C. Ponhea Yat   D. Suryavarman II

15. He was an Indian activist who was leader of the Indian independence movement against British rule. He is well-known for his nonviolent philosophy of passive resistance and his devout Hindu faith.

    A. Jawaharlal Nehru   B. Guru Nanak

    C. Mahatma Gandhi   D. Dalai Lama

Answers - Chapter 6 – Asian Civilizations

1. C – Genghis Khan

2. B – Confucius

3. D – Yu the Great

4. B – Mao Tse Tung (or Chairman Mao)

5. A – Ying Zheng, who after becoming emperor changed his name to Qin Shi Huang

Did You Know: Ying Zheng was born in 259 B.C. He became king of the state of Qin at the age of 13. For the first time in China's history, under his rule China became a unified centralized state and he became China's first emperor. During his time as emperor the Great Wall of China was built and his burial chamber was surrounded by the famous Terracotta Army.

Did You Know: In 1974 a farmer and other peasants outside the city of Xi'an in China while digging a well discovered a life-size clay soldier poised for battle. What he had unearthed would soon prove to be one of the greatest archeological discoveries in the world. Archeologists were called in and they found not one, but thousands of clay soldiers, each with unique facial expressions and positioned according to rank. As a result, each terra cotta soldier appears to be unique in its facial features, revealing a high level of craftsmanship and artistry. Not only were soldiers unearthed, but archers, horses and chariots were stationed in military formation near Emperor Qin's (the first emperor of China) tomb in order to protect the emperor in the afterlife. He lived during the time of the Warring States Period when constant conflict and ceaseless warfare were a part of life. During excavation of the pits containing the terracotta warriors, archaeologists have found some 40,000 bronze weapons, including battle axes, crossbows, arrowheads and spears. Even after more than 2,000 years, these weapons remained extremely well preserved. Archaeologists estimate that there are about 8,000 terracotta figures in the areas surrounding Qin Shihuang's tomb, including horses, archers, charioteers, infantry, and generals. Most of the terracotta warriors are over six feet tall, substantially larger than the average citizen of the Qin Empire at the time. The terracotta army is just one part of Qin Shihuangdi's tomb. Over the past 35 years, archaeologists have located some 600 pits, a complex of underground vaults as yet largely unexcavated, including the tomb of the Emperor himself, which considering the terracotta soldiers protecting his tomb promises to unveil great treasures. Even 40 years after its discovery, less than 1 percent of Emperor Qin's tomb has been excavated. According to Siam Qian, a historian of the Han dynasty, "The tomb was filled with models of palaces, pavilions and offices as well as fine vessels, precious stones and rarities." The account indicates the tomb contains replicas of the area's rivers and streams flowing to the sea through hills and mountains of bronze. Precious stones such as pearls are said to represent the sun, moon, and other stars. Experimental pits dug around the tomb have revealed dancers, musicians, and acrobats full of life and caught in mid-performance, a sharp contrast to the military poses of the famous terracotta soldiers. But for now anyway, the Emperor will remain undisturbed.

6. C – Chiang Kai-shek

7. B – Kublai Khan

8. A – Daoguang

9. D – Puyi

10. C – Oda Nobunaga

11. A – Tokugawa Ieyasu

Did You Know: *Shogun Tokugawa Ieyasu was the de facto ruler of Japan as the government was run under the shogun. The Emperor wouldn't interact with foreigners and as the shogun was the highest ranking position in the noble military class during feudal Japan, it was up to the shogun to interact with Commodore Perry when it came to working on a policy to open the doors to Japan. Tokugawa Ieyasu was the founder and first shogun of the Tokugawa shogunate, or military government, which maintained effective rule over Japan from 1600 until 1867.*

12. B – Murasaki Shikibu

13. A – Kim Jong-un

14. D – Suryavarman II

15. C – Mahatma Gandhi

7

Incan & Aztec Civilizations

Answers for this chapter on page 45

1. What Incan emperor rose to power transforming his kingdom into the largest empire in South America? He was one of Inca's most influential rulers and believed to be the constructor of Machu Picchu.

    A. Pachacuti   B. Manco Cápac II

    C. Atahualpa   D. Túpac Amaru

2. In 1375 he became ruler of the Aztecs. He was the first ruler and founder of the Aztec imperial dynasty.

    A. Tenoch   B. Acamapichtli

    C. Ayaxatla   D. Cotezuma II

3. He was the last of the (independent) rulers of the Aztec empire before the civilization collapsed after the Spanish arrived with Cortes and his men.

    A. Chichimecacihuatzin   B. Montezuma

    C. Ixtlilxochitl   D. Tenoch

Answers - Chapter 7 – Incan & Aztec Civilizations

1. A – Pachacuti
2. C – Acamapichtli
3. B – Montezuma

8

Explorers

Answers for this chapter on page 51

1. A Viking and the son of Erik the Red, he was converted to Christianity by the King of Norway. He is believed to have been the first European to reach the North American continent around the year 1,000 A.D..

    A. *Leif Eriksson*   B. *Rollo of Normandy*

    C. *Gunnar Hamundarson*   D. *Sigmundur Brestisson*

2. In the year 1254 at the age of 15 he began his travels with his father and uncle to the far east. In the year 1275 he met Kublai Khan. He remained in the Khan's service until 1292. After returning to his home in Venice, Italy he joined the army, was captured and imprisoned where he dictated an account of his travels to a fellow prisoner which were later published.

    A. *Amerigo Vespucci*   B. *Vasco Núñez de Balboa*

    C. *Juan Sebastian Elcano*   D. *Marco Polo*

3. In July of 1969 he was the first man to set foot on the moon.

    A. *Gus Grissom*   B. *Buzz Aldrin*

    C. *Neil Armstrong*   D. *Alan Shepard*

4. Under the request of President Thomas Jefferson, what two men led the Corps of Discovery to explore the territories acquired by the U.S. through the Louisiana Purchase?

    A. Livingstone & Stanley   B. Pizarro & Balboa

    C. Hillary & Norgay   D. Lewis & Clark

5. He first sailed to America in 1578 and planned to begin a colony there. It was in 1585 when he established the first English colony on Roanoke Island. He named Virginia after Queen Elizabeth I and the capital of North Carolina was named after him in 1792.

    A. Francis Drake   B. Walter Raleigh

    C. John Cabot   D. John Cabot

6. In 1488 what Portuguese explorer became the first European mariner to round the southern tip of Africa which opened the way for a sea route from Europe to Asia?

    A. Pedro Cabral   B. Afonso Henriques

    C. Bartolomeu Dias   D. Vasco da Gama

7. In 1961 he became not only the first man in space but the first person to orbit the earth.

    A. Yuri Gagarin   B. Alan Shepard

    C. Gus Grissom   D. John Glenn

8. Throughout history there have been brave souls 'going where no man has gone before.' In this case this French explorer explored undersas. He was an ocean explorer producing documentaries on the mysteries of the underwater world.

A. George Bass   B. Mel Fisher

C. Robert Sténuit   D. Jacques Cousteau

9. During the mid-19th century what Scottish missionary and physician is remembered for his explorations of Africa?

A. James Bruce   B. David Livingstone

C. René-Auguste Caillié D. Henry Morton Stanley

10. An Italian explorer, Queen Isabella and King Ferdinand of Spain financed his expedition to sail across the Atlantic to find a direct route to Asia. In 1492 he and his crew sailed off in three ships: the the Santa Maria, the Pinta, and the Niña.

A. James Cook   B. Bartolomew Dias

C. Christopher Columbus D. Juan Sebastian Elcano

11. The continents of North and South America were named after this explorer and navigator who was from Florence, Italy. He played a prominent role in exploring the New World. In 1507 he was the first person to realize the Americas were distinct continents and previously unknown to Europeans, Asians, and Africans.

A. Martin Waldseemuller B. Amerigo Vespucci

C. Juan Ponce de León   D. Roald Amundsen

12. What Portuguese explorer was the first European to reach India by sea?

A. Francisco Pizarro   B. Hernán Cortés

C. Francis Drake   D. Vasco da Gama

13. What Spanish conquistador brought down the Incan Empire?

　　A. Francisco Pizarro　　　　B. Pedro de Alvarado

　　C. Hernán Cortés　　　　　　D. Vasco Nuñez de Balboa

14. What Spanish explorer founded the first European settlement of Puerto Rico and is noted in history as the first European to reach Florida while searching for the Fountain of Youth?

　　A. Hernán Cortés　　　　　　B. Ponce de León

　　C. Hernando de Soto　　　　D. Christopher Columbus

15. He was a participant in the early English slaving voyages to Africa. He had a reputation for piracy against Spanish ships, but was most well-known for his voyage in 1577 to South America when he became the first Englishman to circumnavigate the globe. He was second in command when England defeated the Spanish Armada.

　　A. Zheng He　　　　　　　　B. John Cabot

　　C. Francis Drake　　　　　　D. Henry Hudson

16. What Portuguese explorer left Spain in the year 1519 in search of a western sea route to the Spice Islands? During his voyage he became the first European to cross the Pacific Ocean?

　　A. Jacques Cartier　　　　　B. Christopher Columbus

　　C. Giovanni da Verrazzano　　D. Ferdinand Magellan

17. He was a Spanish explorer and conquistador who took part in the conquests of Central America and Peru. He made a fortune in the Central American slave trade and went on an expedition to conquer Florida for Spain. He and his men were the first Europeans to discover and cross the Mississippi River where he died and was buried.

A. Juan Ponce de León   B. Henry Hudson

C. Hernando de Soto   D. Amerigo Vespucci

18. He was the first European known to have contact with parts of Australia and the Hawaiian Islands. He discovered and charted New Zealand and Australia's Great Barrier Reef and provided the first accurate map of the Pacific.

A. John Cabot   B. James Cook

C. Marco Polo   D. Henry Hudson

19. A French explorer and cartographer, he was best known for establishing and governing settlements in Canada, mapping the St. Lawrence River, founding the city of Quebec, and discovering the Great Lakes. He became known as the 'Father of New France.'

A. Leif Ericson   B. Amerigo Vespucci

C. Samuel de Champlain   D. Jacques Cartier

20. He was an English navigator and explorer hired to find a shorter route to Asia from Europe via the Arctic Ocean. He was twice defeated by ice unable to continue his journey. The third time he chose a southern route going across North America and the Pacific Ocean. While never finding what he was looking for, his voyages did give new information on North America's water routes. A river, a strait, and a bay in North America were named after him.

A. James Cook   B. John Cabot

C. Francis Drake   D. Henry Hudson

Answers - Chapter 8 – Explorers

1. A - Leif Eriksson

2. D – Marco Polo

Did You Know: *When Marco Polo, his father, and his uncle returned to Venice they had a hard time speaking in their native tongues they had been gone so long. Marco had been gone on his travels for the majority of his life. His book greatly influenced geographic exploration and even Christopher Columbus had a copy of his book with him when he sailed off acros the Atlantic in which he wrote annotations in the margins. When Marco Polo was near his death, some who doubted the validity of his tales asked him to recant his story. His reply was he had not even told half of what he had witnessed. His book even today stands among the great records of geographic exploration.*

3. C – Neil Armstrong

4. D – Lewis & Clark

5. B – Walter Raleigh

Did You Know: *He had been a favorite of Queen Elizabeth I until she learned of his secret marriage to one of her maids of honour and had both him and his wife imprisoned in the Tower of London. While imprisoned in the Tower of London he wrote the book, 'History of the World.' He was later released only to be imprisoned again by the queen's successor who had him beheaded for treason. After he was beheaded his head was embalmed and set to his widow in a red leather bag which she carried with her for the rest of her life.*

6. C – Bartolomeu Dias

7. A – Yuri Gagarin

Did You Know: *Gagarin was one of 3,000 applicants to be the first Soviet cosmonaut. He was one of twenty chosen to go through rigorous testing. April 12, 1961 he boarded 'Vostok I' not knowing whether the mission would be successful or not, as no man to date had even been in space. Entering space he orbited the Earth once and then returned to Earth's atmosphere. In all, from the launch to touching down (he ejected and parachuted to Earth) it took 108 minutes. He became an international* hero accomplishing what no other man had done before.

8. D – Jacques Cousteau

Did You Know: *Cousteau co-invented diving and scuba devices including the Aqua-Lung. Before the invention of the Aqua-Lung a heavy diving suit and helmet with a hose that ran to land or to a boat were needed. In 1951, Cousteau began expeditions on the ship the 'Calypso' recording the world of life under the sea. He first became entranced with the mysteries of the sea after being in a car accident that nearly killed him. Part of his rehabilitation to recover from his accident was daily swims in the Mediterranean Sea. A friend gave him a pair of goggles and a whole new world opened up to him. He began a quest to understand the underwater world. During WWII when the Nazis took over Paris he moved close to the Swiss border continuing his underwater explorations. At the same time he was working for the French Resistance for which he received several medals including the Legion of Honor. After the war he helped clear underwater mines and later searched for the Roman shipwreck 'Mahdia,' the first underwater archeology operation using self-contained diving apparatus. He published a book on his underwater explorations, 'The Silent World' and made several television documentaries. He worked hard on a topic he was passionate about, an environmental message to protect the ocean's wildlife habitat. His work helped restrict commercial whaling and underwater dumping of nuclear waste.*

9. B – David Livingstone

Did You Know: *He crossed the continent of Africa from east to west discovering many bodies of water previously uncharted by Europeans – the most well-known being Victoria Falls and the Zambezi River. He became an abolitionist after witnessing the inhumane horrors of the African slave trade. On another journey through Africa while in search of the source of the Nile River he witnessed a massacre where Arabic slave traders killed hundreds from the village of Nyagwe. He died of dysentery and malaria in a village near modern day Zambia. His body was transported toEngland where he was buried at Westminster Abbey.*

10. C – Christopher Columbus

11. - B – Amerigo Vespucci

12. D – Vasco da Gama

13. A – Francisco Pizarro

14. B – Ponce de Leon

15. C – Francis Drake

Did You Know: *On his last voyage, Queen Elizabeth I sent him to the West Indies where he died in Panama of fever and dysentery. He was buried at sea wearing his full armor encased in a lead-lined coffin. Divers and treasure hunters still find his last resting place to be elusive and his remains to this day remain undiscovered.*

16. D – Ferdinand Magellan

17. C – Hernando de Soto

18. B – James Cook

19. C – Samuel de Champlain

20. D – Henry Hudson

Did You Know: *On his last voyage his crew mutinied setting Hudson, his teenage son, and seven of the crew adrift in a small boat. The body of water where they had been set adrift would later be named the Hudson Bay named in his honor. No word was ever heard of their fate.*

9

Pirates & Privateers

Answers for this chapter on page 58

1. He is history's most notorious pirate whose flagships 'La Concorde' was a 200-ton slave ship with 16 cannons which he renamed 'Queen Anne's Revenge.' This remained his primary ship until he wrecked it off the coast of North Carolina.

    A. Captain Morgan   B. Calico Jack Rackham

    C. Blackbeard   D. Captain Kidd

2. He was the most successful pirate during the Golden Age of Piracy.' Originally an officer aboard a slave ship captured by pirates he was forced to join them. In a matter of weeks this 'reluctant' pirate became captain. In three years time he captured and looted over 400 vessels – no other pirate came close to that number. While not the most famous pirate, he was the most successful and the most cruel.

    A. Black Bart   B. Edward England

    C. Black Caesar   D. Long Ben

3. He was considered the most ruthless pirate to roam the seas. Once shipwrecked and under attack he saved his life by smearing blood on his body and hiding among the corpses. He escaped during the night after

freeing some slaves, stealing a boat, and escaping with his new crew. He was known to torture ruthlessly in order to find hidden loot. In Gibraltar alone he killed over 500 men. Waylaid by the Spanish he escaped only to be attacked by a tribe of natives who were cannibals. His end was a gruesome one. As he had shown no mercy, neither did he receive any in the end.

    A. Bartholomew Roberts   B. Stede Bonnet

    C. Jean Lafitte   D. Francois l'Olonnais

4. He earned his fame during the height of the Golden Age of Piracy, not by his wealth in treasure, but he had two female pirates amongst his crew making him stand out as different and memorable. He flew the Jolly Rogers flag, a black flag with a white human skull and two crossed swords beneath it.

    A. Black Caesar   B. Calico Jack Rackham

    C. Captain Kidd   D. Blackbeard

5. A Scottish sea captain, he started out as a privateer who turned pirate. When lack of prizes as a privateer turned him and his crew restless they became pirates capturing treasure ships they wouldn't have been able to touch otherwise and kept all the rewards for themselves. When they captured the 'Queddah Merchant' a treasure ship, they raked in what would be over two million in today's money. Treasure from one of his wrecked ships, 'The Adventure Galley' was discovered which included a 50 kg silver bar.

    A. Long Ben   B. Thomas Tew

    C. Captain Kidd   D. Peter Easton

6. An English pirate who operated in the early 18th century was the wealthiest pirate in history. He called himself 'Robin Hood of the Sea,' and his men called themselves 'Robin Hood's men.' His career as a pirate lasted little more than a year, but in that time he and his crew captured

at least 53 ships and amassed a fortune that today would be valued at $120 million. He never killed a captive and returned the ship and cargo if they didn't suit his purposes. He may have been the wealthiest pirate but his life as a pirate was short-lived. He died in a shipwreck at the age of 28 off the coast of Cape Cod. After the ship sank over 100 bodies were washed ashore and buried in a mass grave by locals. His ship was the 'Whydah Gally,' previously a slave ship captured in 1717 which he refitted as a flagship with 28 guns with an advanced weapons system capable of attacking any man-of-war in the Americas. His ship sank off the coast of Cape Cod with more than four and a half tons of gold and silver.

    A. Black Sam Bellamy   B. Peter Easton

    C. Long Ben   D. Charles Vane

7. In the early 1600's this English pirate with a crew of almost 5,000 amassed a fortune off the coast of Newfoundland and down the eastern coast of America. He earned the title of 'Arch-Pirate' and was the most powerful pirate in the Western Hemisphere. He would receive a pardon and live out his days as a very rich man.

    A. Edward England   B. Samuel Bellamy

    C. Henry Every   D. Peter Easton

8. He is known as the greatest of the privateers. A Welshman, one of his most famous exploits was his attack on Panama in 1671. In 2012 off the coast of Panama his flagship 'Satisfaction' and four other of his ships which had sunk were discovered along with some of his 17th century treasure by Fritz Hanselmann, an underwater archaeologist. This pirate's face can still be seen today on a bottle of his namesake rum.

    A. Captain Kidd   B. Black Bartholomew

    C. Captain Morgan   D. Calico Jack Rackham

9. He remains the most renowned black pirate from a time when a pirate ship was one of the few places a black man could attain power and

wealth. He raided ships in the area of the Florida Keys for about a decade before joining Blackbeard and his crew. Legend has it he buried his treasure on Elliot Key. His treasure was said to include over 26 bars of silver. He ran a brothel and a prison camp with hostages he ransomed off. He met the same fate as many pirates and was hanged.

    A. Black Caesar   B. Thomas Tew

    C. Black Bart   D. Stede Bonnet

10. He was the formidable commander of the Red Flag Fleet of pirate ships. He was a fearsome pirate who operated in the South China Sea during the Qing dynasty. He united many rival Chinese pirate organizations. He married a former prostitute from a floating brothel who after his death succeeded him commanding over 1,800 pirate ships and 80,000 men.

    A. Ching Chelung   B. Cheng I

    C. Pedro Gilbert   D. Benjamin Hornigold

Answers - Chapter 9 – Pirates & Privateers

1. C – Blackbeard

Did You Know: *After the 'Queen Anne's Revenge' sank Blackbeard, or Edward Teach his given name, he approached the governor of North Carolina and asked for a pardon which was granted. He settled down in the town of Bath, married a local woman, and was a frequent dinner guest of his neighbors who found him and his tales fascinating. After a time he returned to his old ways and Virginia's governor planned a way to get rid of this outlaw. After a night of heavy drinking and partying, Naval officer Maynard and his crew attacked Blackbeard and his crew of pirates. Blackbeard went down with 5 shots in him and several cuts in his body from swords. What ended him was the final slash of the sword which cut off his head. Blackbeard's head was mounted on a pole by the Hampton and James Rivers where it remained for several years to warn other pirates they weren't welcome on American soil.*

2. A – Black Bart

3. D – Francois l'Olonnais

4. B – Calico Jack Rackham

5. C – Captain Kidd

Did You Know: *A privateer was commissioned 'legally' to plunder other government's ships and taking their treasures dividing it between the government who commissioned them and keeping some for themselves as payment.*

6. A – Black Sam Bellamy

7. D – Peter Easton

8 – C – Captain Morgan

9 – A – Black Caesar

10 – B – Cheng I

10

Native American Indians

Answers for this chapter on page 64

1. A Nez Perce chief who after white settlers moved onto Indian tribal lands rather than move to a reservation he led his followers in an effort to escape to Canada. He is remembered for saying, "I will fight no more forever."

    A. Chief Joseph   B. Geronimo

    C. Squanto   D. Sitting Bull

2. A Mohawk, he was instrumental in founding the Iroquois Confederacy. Most people are more familiar with him due to Henry Wadsworth Longfellow's poem about him.

    A. Red Cloud   B. Cochise

    C. Pontiac   D. Hiawatha

3. He became the first Native American to win a gold medal at the Olympics. He is remembered as one of the greatest athletes of all time.

    A. Will Rogers   B. Osceola

    C. Jim Thorpe   D. Tecumseh

4. He was a half-Cherokee silversmith who developed a system of writing for the Cherokees. The simplicity of it made it easy to learn and was soon taught to Cherokees throughout the nation. A particular redwood in the Pacific coast was named after him.

    A. Sequoyah   B. Pontiac

    C. Osceola   D. Cochise

5. He killed his first buffalo at age 10 and at age 14 knocked a Crow warrior off his horse with his tomahawk. He was credited with being a brave chief. He was the first man to become chief of the entire Lakota Sioux nation.

    A. Chief Joseph   B. Seattle

    C. Crazy Horse   D. Sitting Bull

6. He was a Cherokee-cowboy who was also an actor, comedian, and presidential candidate.

    A. Jim Thorpe   B. Will Rogers

    C. Black Hawk   D. Sitting Bull

7. A Shawnee chief and brother to The Prophet, he opposed white settlement and was leading the Indian's resistance to white settlers in the Ohio Valley. He was in a battle against William Henry Harrison a future president and military leader at the time and was killed in the War of 1812.

    A. Cochise   B. Pontiac

    C. Tecumseh   D. Osceola

8. This Ottawa chief was known for a rebellion named after him in which the Indians struggled against the British occupation in the Great

Lakes area in 1763 – '64.

    A. Pontiac   B. Black Hawk

    C. Seattle   D. Osceola

9. He was Apache and the son-in-law of Cochise. He hated Mexicans as they raided their camp killing his wife and three children. It was the slaughter of his village and family that turned him from peaceful into a warrior. As the white settlers moved in encroaching on Indian lands he turned against them too. Moved onto a reservation but deprived of traditional tribal rights and short on rations, he along with hundreds of Apaches left the reservation. They began ten years of raids. In 1905 he appeared in President Teddy Roosevelt's parade. In 1906 he dictated the story of his life which was turned into a book.

    A. Sitting Bull   B. Geronimo

    C. Cochise   D. Crazy Horse

10. An Apache chief in an area of southern Arizona and northern Mexico, he resented the encroachment of both Mexican and American settlers and led raids on both sides of the border. He was falsely accused of kidnapping a rancher's son and held against his will. Knowing he was innocent he refused to be held and used a knife to cut his way out of the tent he was being held in and escaped. Years after his death the kidnapped boy resurfaced as an Apache-speaking scout for the U.S. Army and confirmed the Indian's story that he had been innocent of the kidnapping.

    A. Red Cloud   B. Crazy Horse

    C. Chief Powhatan   D. Cochise

11. Captured by European explorers in the early 1600's he was taken to Europe where he learned to speak the English language. He returned to America. He is most remembered for helping the Pilgrims. It is largely due to the aid he gave the Pilgrims that many survived that first winter.

A. Squanto   B. Chief Powhatan

C. Pontiac   D. Tecumseh

12. A chief of the Oglala Lakota tribe, he is remembered for his success in confrontations with the U.S. government. He fought to save his people's lands and was instrumental in organizing resistance to white expansion into American Indian lands. While he resisted the government's efforts to remove him and his people from their lands when gold was discovered in the Black Hills, this brought war to the plains and the end of life as the Indian people had always known. He spent the last years of his life at Pine Ridge Reservation living to the age of 87.

A. Black Hawk   B. Geronimo

C. Red Cloud   D. Sitting Bull

13. A war chief of the Seminoles in Florida and a medicine man he opposed relocation and is viewed as a major figure in securing the rights of the Seminoles, not through treaties but through guerilla warfare. He was captured by American troops under a white flag of truce – one of America's black marks in American military history and also in their dealings with the American Indians.

A. Seminole   B. Osceola

C. Sequoiah   D. Seattle

14. A Lakota Sioux, he was chief who took part in the Battle of Little Big Horn. In the Black Hills of South Dakota is an ongoing project of a monumental sculpture of him which was begun in 1948. Once complete this will be the largest mountain carving in the world, a sculpture of him sitting on his horse.

A. Crazy Horse   B. Geronimo

C. Sitting Bull   D. Cochise

15. He was the principal chief who had to lead his people the Cherokees 1,000 miles from their homelands on the march which came to be known as the 'Trail of Tears.'

    A. Tecumseh   B. Chief John Ross

    C. Chief Joseph   D. Chief Powhatan

Answers - Chapter 10 – Native American Indians

1. A – Chief Joseph

2. D – Hiawatha

3. C – Jim Thorpe

Did You Know: *He won gold medals in the 1912 Olympics in both the pentathlon and the decathlon. He went on to play professional baseball and football and was voted 'the greatest athlete of the half-century' in 1950. He would later be stripped of his Olympic medals due to having previously played minor summer league baseball. Thirty years after his death and seventy years after the medals had been taken from him the medals were restored posthumously.*

4. A – Sequoyah

5. D – Sitting Bull

6. B – Will Rogers

7. C – Tecumseh

8. A – Pontiac

9. B – Geronimo

10. D – Cochise

11. A – Squanto

12. C – Red Cloud

13. B – Osceola

14. A – Crazy Horse

15. B – Chief John Ross

11

Early American History

From year 1000 A.D. - 1800's

Answers for this chapter on page 82

1. (C. 1000 A.D.) He was the first known European to have discovered the continent of North America, nearly 500 years before Christopher Columbus made it to the American continent.

    A. Ponce de Leon   B. Kennewick Man

    C. Leif Erikson   D. Erik the Red

2. (1585) This Englishman, a favorite of Queen Elizabeth I, became famous for establishing the first British colony in America, which was Roanoke Island.

    A. John White   B. Walter Raleigh

    C. Giovanni Verrazzano   D. John Smith

3. In 1586 he was sent by Sir Walter Raleigh as Sir Richard Grenville's artist-illustrator on his first voyage to the New World. In 1587 he served as governor of a second failed expedition which came to be known as the Lost Colony.

    A. James Audubon   B. Phillip Amadas

    C. John White   D. William Bradford

4. What Englishman was captain of the ship the '*Susan Constant*,' the largest of the three ships that brought settlers to the New World who began the settlement of Jamestown in 1606?

    A. Christopher Newport   B. Christopher Jones

    C. Jack Sparrow   D. Francis Drake

5. He was captain of the ship '*Discovery*,' one of the three ships that brought the colonists to the New World in 1607. (They left England in 1606.) He became the second president of the Jamestown colony and was killed by the Pamunkey Native American Indians.

    A. James Cook   B. William Bligh

    C. James Smith   D. John Ratcliffe

6. (1608) He became president of the Jamestown colony and was a strong leader and though in large part it was due to him that as many of the settlers survived that did, few of them liked him. As a legend that has endured for over 400 years goes, his life was saved by a young Indian girl who went by the name Matoaka. She later received the nickname which most of us are more familiar with, Pocahontas meaning playful one.

    A. John Smith   B. Thomas Rolfe

    C. William Brewster   D. George Percy

7. He was an early Englishman settler who arrived in Jamestown in 1610 who developed Virginia's first profitable crop to export – tobacco. Four years after his arrival in Jamestown he married Pocahontas who by that time had converted to Christianity and changed her name to Rebecca.

    A. Nathaniel Powell   B. John Ratcliffe

    C. John Rolfe   D. Nicholas Hancock

8. (1620) He was the captain of the Mayflower during the Pilgrims voyage when they were brought to America.

    A. Gilbert Winslow   *B. William Latham*

    C. Wrestling Brewster   *D. Christopher Jones*

9. He was the only child born on the Mayflower during the voyage. He was born in 1620 and died in 1623.

    A. Love Brewster   *B. Resolved White*

    C. Oceanus Hopkins   *D. Remember Allerton*

10. (1620) He was the first baby boy born on the Mayflower in the harbor of Massachusetts, the second baby born on the Mayflower, and the first English child born to the Pilgrims in the New World.

    A. John Billington   *B. Peregrine White*

    C. Wrestling Brewster   *D. Giles Hopkins*

11. (1620) He is given credit for not only being the first to sign the Mayflower Compact but also for writing it.

    A. John Carver   *B. John Winslow*

    C. Myles Standish   *D. William Brewster*

12. He came on the Mayflower with the Pilgrims to serve as a military leader which position he kept until his death.

    A. John Alden   *B. Stephen Hopkins*

    C. John Smith   *D. Myles Standish*

13. He was one of the founders of Jamestown, helped draft and signed the Mayflower Compact, and was elected the second governor of Jamestown after the first one died. He held that position for 31 years. He wrote the chronicles of the settlement titled *Of Plymouth Plantation.*

    A. William Bradford   B. Stephen Hopkins

    C. Edward Winslow   D. John Billington

14. A Mayflower pilgrim and signer of the Mayflower Compact, his passage on the Mayflower came in exchange with an agreement that he and his family would work on behalf of the colony. Trouble began while still on board the Mayflower when his son almost blew up the ship. He became America's first (recorded) murderer and hung.

    A. John Carver   B. Isaac Allerton

    C. John Billington   D. William White

15. A Separatist, he fled England due to persecution and in Holland ran a printing press publishing religious material where he soon found himself being pursued by the Dutch authorities. He evaded them and as an Elder of the church was chosen to sail on the Mayflower where he then lived at Plymouth Colony dying in 1644 at nearly 80 years of age.

    A. William Bradford   B. John Alden

    C. Myles Standish   D. William Brewster

16. (1621) He was the first Native American to make contact with the Pilgrims. He wandered into Plymouth Colony and much to their surprise he greeted them in English.

    A. Chief Powhatan   B. Samoset

    C. Squanto   D. Pontiac

17. He was a Native American who had been kidnapped twice by English explorers and taken to Spain and sold as a slave. He escaped and returned to America in 1619. He became an interpreter and guide for the Pilgrim settlers at Plymouth. He celebrated the first Thanksgiving with the Pilgrims and American Indians of the Wampanoag tribe.

    A. Osceola   B. Squanto

    C. Powhatan   D. Geronimo

18. He was a Wampanoag chief in the early 1600's who encouraged friendship between the white settlers and the Native Americans. He remained on friendly terms with the Pilgrims and revealed to them a plot by the Massachusetts Indians to attack them. With his forewarning the Pilgrims were able to defeat the plot before it took place.

    A. Massasoit   B. The Prophet

    C. Sequoia   D. Opchanacanough

19. He was a prominent member of Plymouth Colony, was among those who went on early explorations of Cape Cod, traveled with the Indians, and wrote several accounts of the early years at Plymouth Colony. He was assistant to William Bradford and governor of Plymouth.

    A. John Alden   B. Edward Winslow

    C. Myles Standish   D. Stephen Hopkins

20. (1621) He is remembered not only for coming to the New World on the Mayflower, but his courtship to Priscilla Alden which was made famous in Henry Wadsworth Longfellow's poem. They married and had 11 children. He was the last male survivor of the Mayflower passengers.

    A. Myles Standish   B. Isaac Allerton

    C. John Alden   D. John Billington

21. (1636) He was a religious leader, he preached at Salem and Plymouth, was the founder of the colony of Rhode Island and was banished from Massachusetts.

    A. John Clarke   B. Roger Williams

    C. John Leland   D. William Hutchinson

22. He was the first colonist of the Virginia colony known as the instigator in a rebellion which took place in 1676.

    A. John Brown   B. Daniel Shays

    C. Jesse James   D. Nathaniel Bacon

23. (1682) He was a Quaker and founder of the province of Pennsylvania.

    A. John Winthrop   B. George Calvert

    C. William Penn   D. Roger Williams

24. (1692) He was a colonist and a Puritan minister who was involved in governing the Massachusetts Bay Colony. He received a bachelor's degree at the age of 17 and served as president of Harvard in the late 1600's. He was involved in the Salem Witch Trials and had a son who was also a religious leader.

    A. Increase Mather   B. Cotton Mather

    C. Roger Williams   D. Billy Sunday

25. (1770) An African-American, he is considered the first casualty of the American Revolution as he was killed during the Boston Massacre on March 5, 1770.

    A. Crispus Attucks   B. Primus Hall

C. Salem Poor   D. Prince Whipple

26. Who was the Founding Father who was a leader for the movement for America's independence who served as lawyer for the British who fired on the colonists during the Boston Massacre?

    A. Patrick Henry   B. John Adams

    C. Sam Adams   D. Josiah Quincy II

27. Who was the lawyer who was the principal spokesman for the Sons of Liberty in Boston prior to the Revolutionary War? He also served as co-counsel defending British Captain Thomas Preston and the British soldiers involved in the British Massacre.

    A. Josiah Quincy II   B. Thomas Jefferson

    C. John Hancock   D. Thomas Paine

28. Who is known for saying, "Give Me Liberty or Give Me Death"? He was a brilliant orator, a major figure of the American Revolution whose criticisms helped bring about the amendments that became the Bill of Rights. He is most famous for his speech to the Virginia Assembly in 1775 where he said the famous words above.

    A. Thomas Paine   B. John Hancock

    C. Patrick Henry   D. Nathan Hale

29. He was a Founding Father (the oldest Founding Father) and member of the Second Continental Congress, a printer, scientist, inventor, and diplomat. He helped draft the Declaration of Independence and the Constitution, and he negotiated the 1783 Treaty of Paris officially ending the Revolutionary War.

    A. Thomas Jefferson   B. Benjamin Franklin

C. John Adams   D. Sam Adams

30. (1775) His claim to fame was his 'midnight ride' made famous by the Henry Wadsworth Longfellow's poem.

     A. Joseph Warren   B. Ethan Allen

     C. John Paul Jones   D. Paul Revere

31. Who was King of Great Britain during the Revolutionary War?

     A. Henry VIII   B. William IV

     C. George III   C. Philip

32. Who was Commander-in-chief for the Continental Army during the Revolutionary War.?

     A. Nathanael Greene   B. George Washington

     C. Henry Knox   D. Thomas Gage

33. He was a bookstore owner who studied books about military strategy and was a volunteer at Bunker Hill. He developed a friendship with Washington who confided to him the army's need of artillery. This man's idea was to use the cannons from Fort Ticonderoga and have them brought from New York to Boston by using sleds. Once the cannons were in place the British withdrew.

     A. Ethan Allen   B. Crispus Attucks

     C. Horatio Gates   D. Henry Knox

34. He was a French nobleman who fought in America's Revolutionary War. He became an honorary American citizen.

A. George III   B. Louis XVI

C. Marquis de Lafayette   D. Jean-Baptiste Donatien de Vimeur

35. He was an African American who served in the Continental Army under Marquis de Lafayette. He was a double agent and fed the British false information while aiding the colonists with accurate information.

A. James Armistead Lafayette   B. Crispus Attucks

C. Cotton Mather   D. Benjamin Banneker

36. The Prussian officer who served the cause of American independence by converting the Revolutionary Army into a well-trained, disciplined army.

A. Benedict Arnold   B. William Howe

C. Baron von Steuben   D. Banastre Tarleton

37. He was the British general who successfully commanded all of the British forces in the American colonies during the Revolutionary War.

A. John André   B. Thomas Gage

C. William Howe   D. Lord North

38. He was Commander-in-chief of the British army during the Revolutionary War.

A. Lord North   B. Thomas Gage

C. Horatio Gates   D. William Howe

39. He was a British general during the Revolutionary War.

A. Henry Clinton   B. John André

C. Oliver Cromwell   D. Francis Marion

40. He was a Mohawk Indian chief who was a British military officer during the Revolutionary War.

A. Tecumseh   B. Joseph Brant

C. Pontiac   D. Chief Black Kettle

41. Brigadier General during the Revolutionary War, his military career began with the French and Indian War. In the Continental Army he helped defend South Carolina where his elusive warfare tactics helped ensure the colonists victory over the British earning him the nickname 'The Swamp Fox.'

A. Francis Marion   B. John Paul Jones

C. Nathan Hale   D. Ethan Allen

42. He was a Revolutionary War hero who led the Green Mountain Boys to capture Fort Ticonderoga and was the founder of the state of Vermont.

A. Ira Allen   B. Seth Warner

C. Ethan Allen   D. Remember Baker

43. A graduate of Yale who was an officer for the Continental Army during the Revolutionary War, he crossed enemy lines disguised as a teacher to spy on British troops. He was caught and hanged. His last words were, "I only regret that I have but one life to lose for my country."

A. John Paul Jones   B. Nathan Hale

C. Benedict Arnold   D. John Trumbell

44. He served in the British Army for 24 years. He fought in the French Indian War and was a general in the Revolutionary War fighting with the colonists. He is known for his victory at the Battle of Saratoga which turned the tide of victory and for his disgrace at Camden. He is known for being ambitious. He tried to compete with George Washington by attempting to replace him as Commander-in-chief, which as history tells us his attempts were unsuccessful. While he had military experience he wasn't very brave or a good leader.

    A. Benedict Arnold   B. John Burgoyne

    C. Richard Lee   D. Horatio Gates

45. He was a leading member of the Culper Spy Ring who spied for General George Washington during the Revolutionary War and nearly got himself hung. He operated under the code name Samuel Culper.

    A. Abraham Woodhull   B. John André

    C› Benedict Arnold   D. Nathan Hale

46. He was a naval hero during the Revolutionary War known for his victories against British ships.

    A. Abraham Whipple   B. John Paul Jones

    C. Samuel Graves   D. Nicholas Biddle

47. He was an American hero early in the Revolutionary War who later became the most famous traitor in American history.

    A. Nathan Hale   B. Sam Adams

    C. Benedict Arnold   D. Robert Hanssen

48. American artist during the period of the Revolutionary War, notable for his historic paintings. He is known as the 'Painter of the Revolution.'

A. Gilbert Stuart   B. John Trumbull

C. John Singleton Copley   D. Charles Wilson Peale

49. He was a soldier, revolutionary, and farmer who was famous for being a leader of a rebellion in his name, an uprising against debt and tax collection.

A. Daniel Shays   B. Nat Turner

C. Nathaniel Bacon   D. Jacob Leisler

50. (1789) A Founding Father, he was an eyewitness to many of the events that led to the creation of the United States. He opposed the passage of the Constitution not agreeing to it until the Bill of Rights was added.

A. Thomas Jefferson   B. James Madison

C. Alexander Hamilton   D. James Monroe

51. (1789) He was our nation's first president and is known as the 'Father of the Country.'

A. Thomas Jefferson   B. George Washington

C> Benjamin Franklin   D. Samuel Adams

52. (1804) Few of America's founders had as much political influence as this man. He was a member of the Continental Congress, an author of the Federalist papers, first Secretary of Treasury, and one of the founders of the first national bank. Unfortunately, his life was cut short when he was killed in history's most famous duel.

A. Aaron Burr   B. Stephen Douglas

C. Alexander Hamilton   D. Samuel Adams

53. (1804) What two men led the Corps of Discovery throughout the lands of America exploring lands acquired by the United States from the Louisiana Purchase?

    A. Lewis & Clark   B. Livingstone & Stanley

    C. Laurel & Hardy   D. Holmes & Watson

54. (1810) He was a Founding Father, Father of the Constitution, and Architect of the Bill of Rights, who would one day become President of the United States. He is attributed to saying, "If Tyranny and Oppression come to this land, it will be in the guise of fighting a foreign enemy."

    A. John Adams   B. James Madison

    C. Thomas Jefferson   D. James Monroe

55. (1814) He is the author of the 'Star Spangled Banner.'

    A. Samuel Francis Smith   B. John Newton

    C. Francis Scott Key   D. Samuel Francis Smith

56. (1817) He was largely responsible for the construction of the Erie Canal which connected the Hudson River to the Great Lakes.

    A. DeWitt Clinton   B. Robert Fulton

    C. John Findlay Wallace   D. Francis Trenholm Crowe

57. (1836) He was Commander of the Alamo where he lost his life. Legend has it he drew a line in the sand challenging those defending the Alamo to cross the line and fight to the death.

    A. Sam Houston   B. William Travis

    C. Jim Bowie   D. Davy Crockett

58. Mostly remembered for his part in the Alamo, he was also a frontiersman, slave trader, smuggler, he killed a man in a duel, and he was a soldier. He is also known for having a hunting knife named after him. He may have had a dubious past history, yet he is still considered one of the nation's heroes in large part due to his role at the Alamo.

    A. Jim Bowie   B. Davy Crockett

    C. Sam Houston   D. William Travis

59. He is often referred to as 'King of the Wild Frontier.' He was a frontiersman and defender of the Alamo. He represented Tennessee in the U.S. House of Representatives. He is one of the most celebrated and mythologized figures in American history.

    A. Jedidah Smith   B. Davy Crockett

    C. Kit Carson   D. John Colter

60. He played a crucial role in the founding of Texas and became the first president of the Lone Star Republic. It was through his efforts the U.S. recognized Texas gaining it's statehood.

    A. Robert Cavelier   B. Stephen Austin

    C. Santa Anna   D. Sam Houston

61. He was one of only two men who served as Secretary of State under three different presidents – William H. Harrison, John Tyler, and Millard Fillmore. He gained his fame as a champion for a strong federal government.

    A. John Marhsall   B. Henry Clay

    C. Daniel Webster   D. William Seward

62. (1858) A senator from Illinois he was the designer of the Kansas-

Nebraska Act, but is most remembered for his debate with Abraham Lincoln who defeated him in the presidential race.

    A. Stephen Douglas   B. George McClellan

    C. John Breckinridge   D. John Bell

63. (1859) A civil rights activist who believed in the overthrow of slavery. He led his own army of radical abolitionists whose goal was to instigate rebellion among the slaves. He and his followers raided Harper's Ferry military arsenal. He was captured, convicted of treason, and hanged.

    A. Frederick Douglass   B. Martin Luther King, Jr.

    C. James Armistead Lafayette   D. John Brown

64. (1861) A Confederate general, he ordered the first shots of the Civil War at Fort Sumter.

    A. Braxton Bragg   B. P.G.T. Beauregard

    C. Robert Anderson   D. Porter Alexander

65. He served as the only President of the Confederate States during the Civil War.

    A. Robert E. Lee   B. Stonewall Jackson

    C. Jefferson Davis   D. James Longstreet

66. He served as Commander in Chief of the Union Army during the Civil War, leading the North to victory.

    A. Robert E. Lee   B. Winfield Scott

    C. George McClellan   D. Ulysses S. Grant

67. He was a Confederate general who was known for his fearlessness. He earned his nickname at the first Battle of Bull Run for standing fearlessly against enemy fire.

    A. Stonewall Jackson   B. Unconditional Surrender Grant

    C. Hancock "the Superb"   D. Old Flintlock Hanson

68. They were the best-known of the guerilla warfare fighters who fought in the Civil War. The group was named after their leader and included Jesse James and his brother Frank in the group.

    A. Jayhawkers   B. Quantrill's Raiders

    C. McNeill Rangers   D. Mosby's Rangers

69. He was Commander of the Union Army of the Potomac who played a critical role in the Civil War by achieving a major victory at the Battle of Gettysburg crippling the Confederate Army, though he was criticized for allowing General Lee's army to escape to Virginia.

    A. John Buford   B. Ambrose Burnside

    C. Joshua Chamberlain   D. George Meade

70. American Civil War general for the Union Army known for laying waste to the South.

    A. Rufus Dawes   B. William Tecumseh Sherman

    C. Philip Sheridan   D. William "Bloody Bill" Anderson

71. Even though he was General of the Confederate States of America and lost the war, he was the most widely respected of all Civil War commanders.

    A. Robert E. Lee   B. J.E.B. Stuart

C. George Pickett   D. James Longstreet

72. (1865) He assassinated President Abraham Lincoln while the president and the first lady attended a play at Ford's Theater on April 14, 1865.

   A. Charles J. Guiteau   B. Richard Lawrence

   C. John Wilkes Booth   D. John Hinckley, Jr.

73. (1867) As Secretary of State he negotiated the treaty with Russia to purchase Alaska.

   A. Timothy Pickering   B. William Seward

   C. John Marshall   D. Henry Clay

74. (1876) A cavalry command and Indian fighter, he is best remembered for leading 260 of his men to their deaths in the Battle of the Bighorn in 1876.

   A. George Custer   B. Marcus A. Reno

   C. Frederick W. Benteen   D. Philip Henry Sheridan

75. He is the Lakota warrior who is best-known throughout history as the chief who defeated General Custer in the Battle of the Little Bighorn.

   A. Crazy Horse   B. Sitting Bull

   C. White Bull   D. Little Big Man

Answers - Chapter 11 – Early American History

1. C – Leif Erikson

Did You Know: Years ago we were taught that Christopher Columbus was the first European to reach the Americas, and then discoveries were made about Erikson and Vikings who had made it to North America almost 500 years before Columbus. Who knows, perhaps history will be re-written yet again with the discovery of the Kennewick Man skeleton found in the Columbia River that was dated from nearly 8,500 years ago. While not of European descent, he certainly seems to have arrived on American soil long before it had been previously calculated that Native Americans first arrived. A complete genome study of the DNA of the Kennewick Man skeleton show his genes to be more closely related to Native Americans than European or Asian, but the results did not show him as a direct ancestor of any tribe living today. It appears we still have a lot to discover on the history of the early inhabitants of North America.

2. B - Walter Raleigh

3 – C – John White

4. A – Christopher Newport

5. D – John Ratcliffe

Did You Know: The Powhatan Indians had promised the starving colonists they would be given corn, but it was a trap. The colonists were ambushed. Ratcliffe was tied to a stake in front of a fire. The women of the Powhatan tribe removed the skin from his entire body with mussel shells throwing his skin into the fire, even skinning his face and then burned him at the stake.

6. A – John Smith

Did You Know: Many of the settlers who arrived weren't used to hard work in their old lives and they didn't want to work. John Smith's rule was, "If you don't work, you don't eat." They didn't like that, but if he would have relented even more of them would have died of starvation.

7. C – John Rolfe

8. D – Christopher Jones

9. C – Oceanus Hopkins

10. B – Peregrine White

11. A – John Carver

Did You Know: He acted as governor on the Mayflower voyage and once on land he was elected as the first governor of the Plymouth colony from 1620 until his death in 1621.

12. D – Myles Standish

13. A – William Bradford

14. C – John Billington

15. D – William Brewster

16. B – Samoset

17. B – Squanto

Did You Know: The Native Americans who lived in the vicinity of the Plymouth Colony were the Wampanoag. One of them who helped the Pilgrims was Squanto who spoke English. Years previously he had been kidnapped and taken to Europe where he was sold as a slave. He escaped and returned to New England. Upon his return he discovered his entire tribe of Patuxet tribe had been wiped out by smallpox so he made his home with the Wampanoags. He was a translator for the Pilgrims and helped them to plant, hunt, and fish. Without his help it's unlikely as many would have survived as did.

18. A – Massasoit

19. B – Edward Winslow

Did You Know: His second marriage was to Susanna White who was the widow of William White who died during the first winter. Theirs was the first marriage in the Plymouth Colony.

20. C – John Alden

Did You Know: The son of Priscilla and John Alden, Captain John Alden, Jr. was a merchant in Boston and was one of the accused during the Salem Witch Trials. The girls who accused him had never even seen him before, but rumors had spread that he sold ammunition and goods to the Indians during King Williams War. One of the girls who had accused him lost her parents who died in an Indian attack and she blamed him for their deaths. The city was out-of-control hanging those accused of witchcraft and he knew his fate was not hopeful. He escaped jail and hid out in New York until the hysteria of the witch trials came to an end. He then returned to Salem and his case was dismissed.

21. B – Roger Williams

22. D – Nathaniel Bacon

23. C – William Penn

24. A – Increase Mather

25. A – Crispus Attucks

26. B – John Adams

27. A – Josiah Quincy II

28. C – Patrick Henry

29. B – Benjamin Franklin

30. D – Paul Revere

Did You Know: Paul Revere was a patriot who was a silversmith by trade from Boston. He was a member of the Sons of Liberty a political organization that opposed incendiary tax legislation such as the Stamp Act of 1765 and organized demonstrations against the British. he also took part in the Boston Tea Party, but it was his famous ride on the night of April 18, 1775 to warn John Hancock, Sam Adams, and the local militia of the British forces approaching for which he is most remembered.

Revere was the father of 16 children and a thriving silversmith business. He had much to risk, but he was a true patriot that knew it would take many who were willing to risk their homes and their lives to take a stand they knew was worth fighting for. Paul Revere founded the first patriot intelligence network (a spy ring) on record, a Boston-based group known as the "mechanics." Beginning in 1774, the mechanics, also referred to as the Liberty Boys, spied on British soldiers and met regularly in the Green Dragon Tavern to share information. He had a side job as a courier for the Boston Committee of Public Safety, and he also served as a lieutenant colonel in the

Revolutionary War. After the war he returned to his silversmith business, opened a foundry, and opened the first copper rolling mill in America and created copper sheeting for the U.S.S. Constitution He wrote to Congress on behalf of Deborah Simpson who had disguised herself as a man and fought in the Revolutionary War helping her to receive a pension for her service. He again volunteered his aid during the War of 1812.

31. C – George III

32. B – George Washington

33. D – Henry Knox

Did You Know: Henry Knox became the nation's first Secretary of War and Fort Knox was named after him.

34. C – Marquis de Lafayette

Did You Know: He was a teenage noble Frenchman who learned of the struggle in the American colonies for their independence at a dinner party and decided to aid them through financial means and to volunteer persuading other French officers to join him. The dinner party where he learned of the Revolutionary War was held in honor of the British King George III's brother, the very king who was fighting the colonists. The brother of the king had been condemned due to his choice of a bride and in retaliation he sang the praises of the colonists and convinced Lafayette to fight against the British.

Lafayette had an ancestor who had fought with the army of Joan of Arc and came from a long established military family. His father had fought in the Seven Years War where he lost his life.

When arriving in the colonies Congress turned him down until he offered to serve without pay. He was accepted on Washington's staff with who he would have a lifelong friendship. He was with Washington during his days at Valley Forge. For a time he returned to France where he was able to secure additional French troops, supplies, and financial aid.

Years after the war he returned to America and visited the Washingtons at Mount Vernon. His only son was named after George Washington. When Lafayette passed away he was buried in France underneath dirt from Bunker Hill so he would be buried in French and American soil. He had taken the dirt from Bunker Hill when he laid the cornerstone to the monument in 1825. That same monument remains there today.

Lafayette was a hero of two worlds.

35. A – James Armistead Lafayette (not to be confused with Marquis de Lafayette)

Did You Know: *When he joined the Continental army he was a slave but had joined with the permission of his owner. After the war unlike many slaves who had fought who were freed, he returned to his owner and it wasn't until 1787 when he finally won his freedom due in large part to the Marquis de Lafayette whose surname he adopted.*

36. C – Baron von Steuben

Did You Know: *Well trained in the Prussian army where he even served for a time as aide-de-camp to Frederick the Great. It was through a nonexistant lineage and falsified papers that he began using the title of Baron. He had been accused of alleged homosexuality that sent him seeking employment elsewhere. Initially turning him down, after a time Benjamin Franklin sent him to the colonies with a letter of recommendation as he had been impressed with his military skills. Congress sent him to General George Washington at Valley Forge. Communication was a problem as he spoke through a translater. Washington impressed with his skills sent him to oversee the training of his men who were desperately in need of military training. He trained the men and wrote training manuals which were used even through the War of 1812.*

37. B – Thomas Gage

38. D – William Howe

39. A – Henry Clinton

40. B – Joseph Brant

41. A – Francis Marion

42. C – Ethan Allen

43. B – Nathan Hale

44. D – Horatio Gates

45. A – Abraham Woodhull

Did You Know: *The Culper Spy Ring was General Washington's most successful covert spy ring. It is believed they are the ones who uncovered the treasonous acts of*

Benedict Arnold.

46. B – John Paul Jones

Did You Know: In 1779 he was given command over a large ship he renamed the 'Bonhomme Richard' in honor of his friend Benjamin Franklin, author and publisher of 'Poor Richard's Almanack.' Jones famous quote was, "I have not yet begun to fight."

47. C – Benedict Arnold

48. B – John Trumbull

49. A – Daniel Shays

50. D – James Monroe

Did You Know: This future president was a college student at William and Mary but left college to fight in the Revolutionary War. A lieutenant who was with Washington at the crossing of the Delaware River to fight in the Battle of Trenton he suffered a near fatal wound. He also suffered first hand the harsh winters at Valley Forge.

51. B – George Washington

52. C – Alexander Hamilton

Did You Know: His son was killed in a duel in 1801 while attempting to defend his father's honor. In 1804 Alexander Hamilton was killed by Aaron Burr in the most famous duel in history.

53. A – Lewis & Clark

54. B – James Madison

55. C – Francis Scott Key

Did You Know: Are you familiar with the story behind how the 'Star Spangled Banner' came to be written? Francis Scott Key, a lawyer was onboard the British ship HMS Tonnant sent on a mission for a prisoner exchange. He had come for the release of Dr. William Beanes, a prominent physician who had become a prisoner of the British. While onboard Key was treated with respect but was told he wouldn't be permitted to return until after the attack on Baltimore. For 25 hours the British bombarded Fort McHenry. In the early morning dawn the bombardment had ended. Key looked to the fort to see if the American flag still flew. He saw the flag still flying *realizing the British had been defeated. He wrote the words to a poem that would eventually be put to music and renamed 'The Star Spangled Banner,' (he had originally called it 'Defense of Fort McHenry.') and it became our national anthem.*

56. A – DeWitt Clinton

57. B – William Travis

58. A – Jim Bowie

59. B – Davy Crockett

60. D – Sam Houston

61. C – Daniel Webster

62. A – Stephen Douglas

63. D – John Brown

64. B – P.G.T. Beauregard

65. C – Jefferson Davis

Did You Know: *Not only was he named after a Founding Father who became a president Thomas Jefferson, but his first father-in-law would also become president, Zachary Taylor, who had refused to attend his daughter's wedding when they married. She died only months after their marriage of malaria while still on their honeymoon.*

66. D – Ulysses S. Grant

67. A – Stonewall Jackson

68. B – Quantrill's Raiders

69. D – George Meade

70. B – William Tecumseh Sherman

Did You Know: *Sherman's troops left a trail of destruction, the first to carry out what became known as "total war." The destruction his troops left behind was a determining factor in the Confederacy's ability to fight. While even today he is not fondly remembered in the South, he is recognized as a great strategist and along with Ulysses S. Grant, one of the best Union generals who fought in the Civil War.*

71. A – Robert E. Lee

Did You Know: President Lincoln wanted Robert E. Lee to lead the Union troops and while Lee opposed succession as he personally believed that a multiracial culture was possible, a world in which blacks and whites could live together without conflict, (yet today he is erroneously portrayed as a racist), it was due to Lee's loyalty to his state of Virginia why he refused the offer of leading the Union troops.

72. C – John Wilkes Booth

Did You Know: Ironically, Edwin Booth a well-known actor and brother of John Wilkes Booth saved the life of Abraham Lincoln's oldest son Robert just months before his brother assassinated Robert's father, the president. Waiting on the railway platform for his train Robert was accidently pushed into the path of an oncoming train with no way to save himself. Booth seized the collar of the president's son and pulled him to safety. While Robert Lincoln recognized his rescuer a well-known actor, Edwin did not know who Robert was at that time. Edwin Booth did not share his brother's hatred for the president. He had voted for him for president.

73. B – William Seward

Did You Know: The purchase of Alaska for $7.2 million worked out to be about 2 cents an acre. While a remarkable purchase, at the time the people called it 'Seward's Folly.'

74. A – George Custer

Did You Know: The battle was also known as 'Custer's Last Stand.' It remains one of the most controversial battles in U.S. History.

75. B – Sitting Bull

12

Founding Fathers

&

Signers of the Declaration of Independence

Answers for this chapter on page 97

1. He was one of Boston's most prominent revolutionary leaders. He was considered the leader of the protest movement against British authority in Massachusetts. With issues of taxation and no representation he led the resistance.

    A. John Hancock   B. John Jay

    C. Samuel Adams   D. Benjamin Franklin

2. He was the author of 'Common Sense' which was a great tool for convincing colonists and the Founding Fathers of the wisdom in rebelling against the British. During the Revolutionary War he wrote 'The Crisis' that inspired the soldiers.

    A. Thomas Paine   B. Robert Morris

C. George Mason   D. John Hancock

3. He was the main author of the Declaration of Independence.

   A. John Adams   B. Thomas Jefferson

   C. Robert Livingstone   D. Roger Sherman

4. Which of the Founding Fathers took up six inches of space when signing his name on the Declaration of Independence? He was the first to sign and he signed with a large, bold signature which would be prominent above all others on this historical document.

   A. Button Gwinnett   B. John Adams

   C. Samuel Adams   D. John Hancock

5. The Declaration of Independence was greatly influenced by his work on the Virginia Bill of Rights. His ideas had a large impact on the development of the Bill of Rights to the Constitution, though he would oppose the Constitution due to compromise concerning slavery and the failure of including a Bill of Rights, so therefore he refused to sign it.

   A. James Madison   B. George Mason

   C. James Monroe   D. Thomas Jefferson

6. He was the oldest of the members of the Second Continental Congress and a member of the Committee of Five, chosen to draft the Declaration of Independence. He made corrections to the original which Thomas Jefferson included in the final copy. He was a key figure in procuring financial aid from France for the revolution and helped to negotiate the Treaty of Paris which officially ended the war.

   A. Roger Sherman   B. John Adams

   C. Benjamin Franklin   D. Robert Livingstone

7. He was the Founding Father that compelled Congress to adopt the Declaration of Independence. He was also one of the Founding Fathers who helped draft the document. He nominated George Washington as the Commander-in-chief. He was a member of the First and the Second Continental Congress, he proposed the colonies each adopt independent governments, and it was he who seconded Richard Lee's resolution of independence.

    A. Samuel Chase   B. John Adams

    C. Elbridge Gerry   D. Benjamin Rush

8. This Founding Father played an important role in helping to finance the American Revolution. He signed the Declaration of Independence, the Constitution, and the Articles of Confederation.

    A. Robert Morris   B. George Wythe

    C. Roger Sherman   D. Samuel Chase

9. He was a member of the First Continental Congress and was chosen to become the Commander-in-Chief of the Continental army. He was president of the Constitutional Convention.

    A. Samuel Adams   B. George Washington

    C. Carter Braxton   D. John Hancock

10. It was his idea that a person be a citizen of the union, not of an individual state.

    A. Button Gwinnett   B. Francis Lightfoot Lee

    C. Benjamin Rush   D. Gouveneur Morris

11. This Founding Father is known as the "Father of the Constitution," the author of the most significant legal document in American history.

A. Thomas Jefferson   B. James Monroe

C. James Madison   D. Benjamin Franklin

12. Which Founding Father was a delegate to the Constitutional Convention, co-authored the Federalist papers, and became the nation's first Secretary of Treasury?

A. Alexander Hamilton   B. Gouveneur Morris

C. James Monroe   D. George Mason

13. This Founding Father served as the first Chief Justice of the U.S. Supreme Court, served as President of the Continental Congress, and signed the Treaty of Paris officially ending the Revolutionary War.

A. Elbridge Gerry   B. George Mason

C. John Jay   D. John Hancock

14. *Choose the two correct answers.* Which two Founding Fathers died on the same day and same year – July 4, 1826, which was the 50th anniversary of the adoption of the Declaration of Independence?

A. James Monroe   B. John Adams

C. Thomas Jefferson   D. James Madison

15. Some consider him the Father of Delaware as he was the author of the state's first Constitution in 1776. He is the only southern statesman who signed all three of the great state papers on which our country's history is based: the Petition to the King of the Congress in 1774 (calling for a repeal to the Intolerable Acts), the Declaration of Independence, and the Constitution. He is the only person who signed the Constitution twice. (He was authorized to sign for fellow delegate John Dickinson who was ill.)

A. Josiah Bartlett   B. George Read

C. Charles Carroll   D. John Witherspoon

16. Similar to Paul Revere, he too is famous for a midnight ride – for independence. A motion had been put forward for the colonies to seek their independence. The vote had taken place and while they had enough votes to go forward, the Continental Congress didn't want to go forward and declare independence without unanimous support. He was one of two delegates from Delaware (the other delegate voted against) and had been away due to serving in the militia. When he received word his vote was desperately needed for independence he rode 80 miles, traveled through a thunderstorm arriving at Independence Hall to cast the decisive note.

A. Caesar Rodney   B. William Whipple

C. Robert Treat Paine   D. George Ross

17. He served in the Continental Congress for one state and served as Chief Justice of another state. It is believed he was the last person to sign the Declaration of Independence.

A. Joseph Hewes   B. Oliver Wolcott

C. Thomas McKean   D. Stephen Hopkins

18. He was one of the first to support the idea of complete independence from Great Britain. He was one of five who signed both the Declaration of Independence and the Constitution.

A. Robert Morris   B. George Clymer

C. Elbridge Gerry   D. Samuel Huntington

19. You might remember this signer due to his odd name. His signature is the most valued of all the signers and the rarest to come by. One of his

signatures sold in a 2013 New York auction for $722,000. He was only one of two signers who were born in England. He died in a duel with a political rival in 1777 (hence the rarity of his signature).

    A. William Whipple   B. Button Gwinnett

    C. William Williams   D. Francis Lightfoot Lee

20. He was the first to vote for independence during the Continental Congress in 1775 and is believed to be the second to have signed the Declaration of Independence.

    A. Josiah Bartlett   B. John Hancock

    C. Benjamin Franklin   D. Samuel Adams

21. He was cousin to Benedict Arnold, our nation's most infamous traitor. He, along with Benjamin Franklin, was one of the oldest signers of the Declaration of Independence. Suffering from "shaking palsy" made his signature appear shaky. At the time of the signing he stated, "My hand trembles, but my heart does not."

    A. George Wythe   B. Lewis Morris

    C. John Witherspoon   D. Stephen Hopkins

22. He was involved with the Sons of Liberty. He was sent to the Continental Congress to replace another delegate (Samuel Ward) who had died. In regards to the day the Declaration of Independence was signed, he wrote this: "I was determined to see how they all looked as they signed what might be their death warrant. I placed myself beside the Secretary Charles Thomson and eyed each closely as he affixed each name to the document. Undaunted resolution was displayed in every countenance."

    A. Benjamin Franklin   B. Roger Sherman

    C. William Ellery   D. Benjamin Harrison V

23. A Virginia delegate to the Continental Congress, this man had dropped out of college when lightening killed his father and two sisters. His son became our nation's 9th president and his great-grandson the 23rd president.

    A. George Washington   B. John Adams

    C. Benjamin Harrison V   D. Benjamin Franklin

24. A delegate of New Jersey, he was an ardent supporter of the colonies independence. He was a writer and composer writing a number of songs and ballads. Being of artistic mind, unsubstantiated rumor has it that he may have designed the first U.S. flag.

    A. George Read   B. William Ellery

    C. Francis Hopkinson   D. Benjamin Rush

25. After fighting in the French & Indian War, this Continental delegate had no love for the British crown. He was a strong advocate for independence. He readily signed but had this to say about the occasion. "If we fail, I know what my fate will be. I have done much to prosecute the war; and one thing I have done which the British will never pardon – I have signed the Declaration of Independence; I shall be hanged." Another delegate, Benjamin Huntington, of the Second Continental Congress responded, "If we fail, I shall be exempt from the gallows, for my name is not attached to the Declaration, nor have I ever written anything against the British government." The patriot responded to this statement, "Then sir, you deserve to be hanged for not doing your duty." Who was this patriot who minced no words with his fellow delegate?

    A William Williams   B. Thomas McKean

    C. George Read   D. Samuel Adams

Answers - Chapter 12 – Founding Fathers & Signers of the Declaration of Independence

1. C – Samuel Adams

Did You Know: He was one of the founders of the Sons of Liberty and helped organize the Boston Tea Party. He was a member of both the First and Second Continental Congress. Sam and John Adams were 2nd cousins. The only other family members to sign were brothers Richard and Francis Lightfoot Lee.

2. A – Thomas Paine

3. B – Thomas Jefferson

Did You Know: When he wrote the Declaration of Independence he was only thirty three years of age. He wrote it in a rented room taking 17 days to complete it while in seclusion. Congress then took another 2 days to make changes. In his first draft of the Declaration of Independence he called for an end to slavery, but he took it out in fear that if he left it in the document wouldn't be approved by some of the delegates.

4. D – John Hancock

5. B – George Mason

6. C – Benjamin Franklin

7. B – John Adams

Did You Know: In reference to the signing of the Declaration of Independence, John Adams said: "The date will be the most memorable epoch in the history of America. I am apt to believe that it will be celebrated by succeeding generations as the great anniversary festival. It ought to be commemorated as the day of deliverance, by solemn acts of devotion to God Almighty. It ought to be solemnized with pomp and parade, with shows, games, sports, guns, bells, bonfires, and illuminations from one end of the continent to the other. From this time forward forever more."

8. A – Robert Morris

9. B – George Washington

10. D – Gouverneur Morris

11. C – James Madison

12. A – Alexander Hamilton

13. C – John Jay

14. B & C – John Adams & Thomas Jefferson

Did You Know: James Monroe also died on July 4th, but not until the year 1831. Another Founding Father, James Madison, declined the offer to prolong his life so he could also die on this historic day which would have made four out of the five men who were Founding Fathers who also became presidents to complete their lives on a day that was the most important day in the history of our country. When the elderly Madison was on his deathbed in the year 1836, his doctor asked if he would like to take stimulants to keep him alive until July 4th, the same historic date that Jefferson, John Adams, and James Monroe had all perished. Madison turned down the offer and passed away on June 28, six days before the 60th anniversary of the nation's birth. At the time of his death, he was the last surviving signer of the Constitution.

15. B – George Read

16. A – Caesar Rodney

17. C – Thomas McKean

18. B – George Clymer

19. B – Button Gwinnett

20. A – Josiah Bartlett

21. D – Stephen Hopkins

22. C – William Ellery

23. C – Benjamin Harrison V

Did You Know: Harrison's family fled Berkeley Plantation, their home when traitor Benedict Arnold and his men landed their boats and pillaged from Berkeley to Richmond. While at the Berkeley Plantation Arnold's men threw all the Harrison's family portraits in a bonfire and used their cows for target practice. Harrison was a close friend of George Washington. He befriended Patrick Henry and Thomas

Jefferson while attending William & Mary.

24. C – Francis Hopkinson

Did You Know: *While we have all learned in the past that it was Betsy Ross who sewed the American flag (though there is no proof to substantiate this claim), it was believed (but also unproven) that Francis Hopkinson, a delegate of the Continental Congress and a signer of the Declaration of Independence who actually designed the flag. He was artistic and contributed to the design of numerous important symbols and seals for the United States in the nation's infancy. It is believed that he designed our nation's first flag. Though again, there is no way to substantiate this claim as at the time there just wasn't the emphasis put on memorializing this for future generations. He did however write a letter in the year 1780 to the Board of Admiralty in which he made the claim that he designed the American flag. He was writing to them asking for compensation for designing the flag, first requesting a cask of wine and later withdrawing that request and asking for financial payment. Though he was denied payment, the letters between Hopkinson and the Board of Admiralty does give more credence to the claim that he at the very least had a major hand in designing the flag. He also contributed to the design of the Great Seal of the United States.*

25. A – William Williams

13

Civil War

Answers for this chapter on page 106

1. He was president during the Civil War.

    A. James Buchanan   B. Abraham Lincoln

    C. Andrew Johnson   D. Ulysses S. Grant

2. He commanded Fort Sumter during the attack by the Confederate Army – the beginning of the Civil War.

    A. Robert Anderson   B. George Pickett

    C. Joshua Chamberlain   D. Horace Greeley

3. He was President of the Confederate States of America during the Civil War.

    A. Abraham Lincoln   B. Robert E. Lee

    C. Jefferson Davis   D. Stonewall Jackson

4. He was one of the most successful Southern generals during the Civil War. He was a decisive factor in many significant battles for the south

until being mortally wounded by friendly fire.

    A. Ambrose Burnside   B. Stonewall Jackson

    C. Robert Gould Shaw   D. George McClellan

5. A Confederate cavalry commander known for his speed and elusiveness earned the nickname "Gray Ghost."

    A. Matthew Brady   B. Winfield Scott Hancock

    C. Robert Anderson   D. John Mosby

6. One of the most controversial figures of the Civil War era was a cavalry commander often described as a "born military genius," but he also was responsible for the massacre of African American Union troops in the Battle of Fort Pillow – following a Union surrender. (After the war he served as the first Grand Wizard of the Klu Klux Klan.)

    A. Nathan Bedford Forrest   B. John B. Hood

    C. William T. Sherman   D. Philip Sheridan

7. How many men who would later become presidents served in the Civil War? Kudos to you if you can also name them.

    A. 2   B. 3

    C. 4   D. 6

8. A Confederate general during the Civil War who lost a leg and the use of one of his arms at the Battle of Gettysburg and Chickamauga. He was one of the youngest officers on either side to independently lead an army. His division played a significant role at Gettysburg and were a part of the assault at Little Round Top.

    A. Jeb Stuart   B. Philip Sheridan

C. John Bell Hood   D. Nathan Bedford Forrest

9. Commander of the Union Army of the Potomac, his men built fortifications around Washington, D.C. He fought in the Battles of Antietam and Fredericksburg and would achieve a major victory at Gettysburg which crippled the Confederate Army. He was widely criticized for allowing Robert E. Lee's forces to escape and afterward was replaced by Ulysses S. Grant.

   A. George Meade   B. George Pickett

   C. George McClellan   D. Winfield Scott Hancock

10. He led the Union forces in crushing campaigns through the South. He and his troops laid waste in the South. The press labeled him a lunatic. He is the only man to twice receive thanks from Congress during the war – once for his actions at Chattanooga and again for capturing Atlanta and Savannah.

   A. P.G.T. Beauregard   B. William T. Sherman

   C. Joshua Chamberlain   D. Robert Anderson

11. A Confederate general he ordered the first shots of the Civil War during the bombardment of Fort Sumter. He had a hand in the victory for the South at the First Battle of Bull Run. He was instrumental in creating the Confederate flag.

   A. Robert E. Lee   B. Ambrose Burnside

   C. P.G.T. Beauregard   D. Jeb Stuart

12. He was one of the earliest photographers in American history. He was best known for his scenes of the Civil War.

   A. Horace Greeley   B. Joe Rosenthal

  C. Robert Capa   D. Mathew Brady

13. He was a Union general during the Civil War who was known for his unusual style of facial hair. He organized the 1ˢᵗ Rhode Island Infantry, one of the first units to arrive in Washington to protect the capitol. He served in the Union defeat at the First Battle of Bull Run. He was offered command of the Army of the Potomac twice, both times declining citing a lack of experience. He later issued several controversial commands that verified his lack of experience and failed to fully engage his troops failing to distinguish himself as a successful military leader.

  A. Ambrose Burnside   B. Philip Sheridan

  C. John Mosby   D. Robert Gould Shaw

14. Newspaper editor of the New York Tribune who shaped public opinion for decades. He was known specifically for his strong sentiments of antislavery, advocating early emancipation for slaves.

  A. Warren Harding   B. T. C. DeLeon

  C. Horace Greeley   D. August Belmont

15. A Union officer during the Civil War, he was often at odds with President Lincoln due to this officer's reticence and cautious tactics in attacking the Confederate army. He was eventually removed from command. He attempted a presidential bid against President Lincoln in 1864 in which he failed.

  A. Ulysses S. Grant   B. George McClellan

  C. Jefferson Davis   D. Joshua Chamberlain

16. Union general during the Civil War at the Battle of Gettysburg, he commanded the Union soldiers who fought against the Confederates led by his good friend General Armistead during Pickett's charge.

A. Joshua Chamberlain   B. John Bell Hood

C. Philip Sheridan   D. Winfield Scott Hancock

17. One of the foremost Confederate generals of the Civil War, Robert E. Lee called him "his war horse." He became known for his defensive strategies and tactics. Along with Stonewall Jackson, he became one of the most trusted field commanders in Lee's army. The Battle of Gettysburg was one of his most controversial moments of the war.

A. James Longstreet   B. Jeb Stuart

C. P.G.T. Beauregard   D. George Pickett

18. He was a Confederate major general during the Civil War who was best known for his leadership at Gettysburg. His brave men were decimated during a frontal assault.

A. Jeb Stuart   B. P.G.T. Beauregard

C. John Bell Hood   D. George Pickett

19. When his home state of Virginia seceded, he resigned from the U.S. Army to join the Confederate Army. He was promoted to colonel while serving under Stonewall Jackson and soon promoted to major general. With a reputation of being the "eyes and ears" of the Confederate Army, this major general and cavalry commander was one of the Confederate's most prominent figures, though he was partially blamed for the defeat at Gettysburg.

A. John Bell Hood   B. Ambrose Burnside

C. J.E.B. Stuart   D. P.G.T. Beauregard

20. He is best known for his part at the Battle of Gettysburg where he was assigned to hold the Little Round Top. When his men ran low on ammunition he ordered a bayonet charge. For his heroic defense of the

hill he earned the Congressional Medal of Honor.

    A. Joshua Chamberlain   B. George McClellan

    C. Winfield Scott Hancock   D. Robert Gould Shaw

21. He was a leader in the Union Army leading the famous 54th Massachusetts Infantry, one of the first African American regiments in the Civil War. He was portrayed in the Civil War movie 'Glory.'

    A. Philip Sheridan   B. George McClellan

    C. Robert Gould Shaw   D. John Mosby

22. At the Battle of Sayler's Creek he was able to cut off and capture nearly a quarter of General Robert E. Lee's Army. He then blocked Lee's escape and cornered him at Appomattox Courthouse where Lee surrendered.

    A. Mathew Brady   B. George Pickett

    C. Robert Anderson   D. Philip Sheridan

23. He was the commanding general of the Confederate Army during the Civil War.

    A. Jeb Stuart   B. Jefferson Davis

    C. Robert E. Lee   D. James Longstreet

24. He served as Commander in Chief of the Union Army leading the North to victory over the Confederacy in the Civil War.

    A. George McClellan   B. Ulysses S. Grant

    C. William T. Sherman   D. Robert Anderson

Answers - Chapter 13 – Civil War

1. B – Abraham Lincoln

2. A – Robert Anderson

3. C – Jefferson Davis

4. B – Stonewall Jackson

Did You Know: *He earned his nickname of 'Stonewall' at the First Battle of Bull Run when standing against an attack. One of his generals observing him said he was standing like a stone wall.*

5. D – John Mosby

6. A – Nathan Bedford Forrest

7. D – 6

Did You Know: *Of the men who would become presidents who fought in the Civil War, all of these men fought for the Union: Ulysses S. Grant, Rutherford B. Hayes, James Garfield, Chester Arthur, Benjamin Harrison, and William McKinley. Grover Cleveland did **not** serve in the Civil War choosing instead to pay a substitute to take his place. This was legal though controversial, less than honorable and not looked upon very favorably.*

8. C – John Bell Hood

9. A – George Meade

10. B – William T. Sherman

11. C – P.G.T. Beauregard

Did You Know: *He thought the original Confederate flag was too similar to the U.S. flag and it would be confusing during battle, so he was instrumental in creating the Confederate flag.*

12. D – Mathew Brady

13. A – Ambrose Burnside

14. C – Horace Greeley

15. B – George McClellan

16. D – Winfield Scott Hancock

17. A – James Longstreet

18. D – George Pickett

19. C – J.E.B. Stuart

20. A – Joshua Chamberlain

21. C – Robert Gould Shaw

22. D – Philip Sheridan

23. C – Robert E. Lee

24. B – Ulysses S. Grant

14

The Wild West

Answers for this chapter on page 112

1. Legend or real, the stories about him in large part come from fictional tales and dime novels. He was a frontiersman, guide, and trapper who gained his fame as a guide for explorers in the western frontier where America before then only told tales of hostile Indians and unsettled lands. He made valuable contributions to the westward expansion of the U.S.

   A. Sam Bass   B. Wild Bill Hickok

   C. Kit Carson   D. Jeremiah Johnson

2. One of the most well-known gunslingers, he started his life of crime with petty theft and horse thievery. Rumor has it he killed for the first time at the age of 18. It's believed in all he killed 21 men in his lifetime, one for each year of his life, before he himself was killed.

   A. Billy the Kidd   B. Jesse James

   C. Doc Holliday   D. Black Bart

3. This Old West legend was a scout, buffalo hunter, and showman. Killing over 4,000 buffalo earned him his nickname; not for sport but he had been hired by the railroad to supply them with buffalo meat. An

expert shot, he used those skills for starting a Wild West show. He became an international celebrity and one of the most famous men in America.

    A. Bat Masterson   B. Johnny Ringo

    C. Wild Bill Hickok   D. Buffalo Bill Cody

4. He was best known for being a part of the gunfight at the O.K. Corral. He acquired the reputation of being one of the Old West's toughest and deadliest gunmen of his day. In large part the legend of this man came from his own storytelling. He was the last survivor of the participants of the O.K. Corral shootout.

    A. Kit Carson   B. Wyatt Earp

    C. Doc Holliday   D. Bat Masterson

5. He was a good-mannered stagecoach robber who left poetic messages behind after some of his robberies. He was considered a gentleman bandit and one of the most unusual robbers in American history. He never harmed a passenger in his 28 stagecoach robberies.

    A. Billy the Kidd   B. Jesse James

    C. James Younger   D. Black Bart

6. He was one of the most famous of the James Younger Gang. He robbed banks, stagecoaches, and trains. He was a celebrity even before his death. He was shot in the back of the head by a friend he trusted.

    A. Johnny Ringo   B. Wyatt Earp

    C. Jesse James   D. Sam Bass

7. He was a gunfighter, a gambler, and Wyatt Earp's deputy.

A. Bat Masterson   B. Judge Roy Bean

C. Kit Carson   D. Doc Holliday

8. Folk hero of the Wild West, he was a drover, wagon master, soldier, spy, scout, lawman, gun fighter, gambler, and in show business. He is perhaps most noted for being the most famous of all Western gunfighters.

A. Buffalo Bill Cody   B. Wild Bill Hickok

C. Kit Carson   D. Wyatt Earp

9. A legendary frontier judge who ruled by a law book and a six-shooter gun. He once fined a dead man $40 (the exact amount he had in his pocket) for carrying a concealed weapon. He killed a few men himself before learning a Justice of the Peace was needed and became the self-proclaimed "only law west of the Pecos."

A. Judge Roy Bean   B. Sheriff Pat Garrett

C. Seth Bullock   D. William Davis Allison

10. Often dubbed, "Deadly Doctor of the American West," he was a dentist, a gambler, and a gunman. Diagnosed with tuberculosis he moved out west where he befriended Wyatt Earp. It was his friendship with Earp that involved him in the famous shoot-out at the O.K. Corral, the most famous shootout in the history of the American Wild West.

A. Ike Clanton   B. Bat Masterson

C. Virgil Earp   D. Doc Holliday

11. He was a notorious outlaw who fought gun battles and was given the nickname "King of the Cowboys." He was notorious for his deadly fast draw.

A. Black Bart   B. Johnny Ringo

C. Sam Bass   D. Kit Carson

12. He and his gang robbed the Union Pacific gold-train from San Francisco raking in over $60,000 – to this day the largest single robbery of the Union Pacific.

A. Butch Cassidy   B. William Reno

C. Sam Bass   D. Jess Newton

Answers - Chapter 14 – The Wild West

1. C – Kit Carson

2. A – Billy the Kid

3. D – Buffalo Bill Cody

4. B – Wyatt Earp

5. D – Black Bart

6. C – Jesse James

7. A – Bat Masterson

8. B – Wild Bill Hickok

9. A – Judge Roy Bean

10. D – Doc Holliday

11. B – Johnny Ringo

12. C – Sam Bass

15

Bad Guys:
Gangsters, Presidents Assassins, Serial Killers, & Terrorist

Answers for this chapter on page 119

1. He was the most infamous gangster in American history. He worked out of Chicago and was responsible for the St. Valentine's Day Massacre, where he ordered the killings of 7 of his rivals. During Prohibition he brought in $60 million a year selling illegal alcohol. For a time he was imprisoned at Alcatraz.

    A. Lucky Luciano   B. John Dillinger

    C. Al Capone   D. Baby Face Nelson

2. He was perhaps the most famous bank robber in American history and famous for his jail breaks. He met his end by being shot to death by FBI agents.

    A. Carlo Gambino   B. John Dillinger

    C. Meyer Lansky   D. John Gotti

3. This mobster built the Flamingo casino in Las Vegas. While he was never convicted of a serious crime, at one time he tried to sell explosives to Benito Mussolini. His 1947 murder remains unsolved.

   A. Bugsy Siegel   B. Al Capone

   C. Machine Gun Kelly   D. Frank Costello

4. This gangster was remembered for his vicious killings and youthful looks which earned him his nickname everyone remembers him by.

   A. Vito Genovese   B. Baby Face Nelson

   C. Albert Anastasia   D. Bugsy Siegel

5. He was the most powerful boss of organized crime in the early 1930's. He is best known for establishing organized crime in the U.S., the first boss of the modern Genovese crime family.

   A. John Gotti   B. Al Capone

   C. Meyer Lansky   D. Lucky Luciano

6. Head of the Gambino family, this organized crime boss was known as 'Teflon Don' after getting off on federal racketeering charges. He was a prominent figure in the organized crime world in the 1980's and '90's.

   A. Lucky Luciano   B. Tony Accardo

   C. John Gotti   D. Vincent Gigante

7. He was one of America's best-loved bank robbers, as the Oklahoma locals called him "the Robin Hood of the Cookson Hills," as he destroyed mortgage papers when he robbed banks freeing the owners from the debt and he shared the money he robbed. He became Public Enemy #1 and was eventually killed by the FBI. He became a legend when Woody Guthrie wrote a song about him.

A. Pretty Boy Floyd   B. Lucky Luciano

C. Bugsy Siegel   D. John Dillinger

8. Italian-born American gangster boss of the Gambino crime family, he is the Mafia's original Godfather. During his time he was the single most powerful organized crime figure in America and one of the most ruthless.

A. Meyer Lansky   B. Al Capone

C. Frank Costello   D. Carlo Gambino

9. President Lincoln was our first president to be assassinated. An actor, though not of equal standing of his famous brother and father who were also actors, he planned along with friends of his to kill the president, vice-president, and secretary of state. Of the three planned assassinations he was the only one who succeeded when he shot and mortally wounded President Lincoln. Who was President Lincoln's assassin?

A. Lee Harvey Oswald   B. Leon Gzolgosz

C. John Wilkes Booth   D. Charles Guiteau

10. President James Garfield was shot by a man who believed he was given a message from God to kill the president. At the train station with his two oldest sons who witnessed the episode, he was shot in the back and mortally wounded by this assassin.

A. Charles Guiteau   B. John Hinckley, Jr.

C. Everett Dutschke   D. Richard Lawrence

11. President McKinley was assassinated by this man, a member of a radical socialist movement. At the Pan-American Exposition when the president reached to shake this man's hand he fired tiwce at point blank range. The president died 8 days later from gangrene due to the gunshot

wounds. Who assassinated President McKinley?

    A. John Schrank   B. Leon Czolgosz

    C. Giuseppe Zangara   D. Oscar Collazo

12. This man was arrested for assassinating President Kennedy after he was shot and killed in a motorcade in Dallas

    A. Lyndon B. Johnson   B. Charles Voyde Harrelson

    C. CIA   D. Lee Harvey Oswald

13. America's first serial killer in the modern era murdered at least a dozen women in the Boston area in the early 1960's. What was this serial killer's moniker/nickname?

    A. Boston Strangler   B. Zodiac Killer

    C. The Stocking Strangler   D. The Angel of Death

14. Known as the "Gainesville Ripper" and the "Gainesville Slasher," this serial killer murdered five college students in Gainesville, Florida. He confessed to killing 8 people.

    A. Ted Bundy   B. Edmund Kemper

    C. Danny Rolling   D. John Collins

15. A serial killer who pleaded guilty to 8 shootings in New York City in the late 1970's was known as "The Son of Sam."

    A. Wayne Williams   B. David Berkowitz

    C. Vernon Butts   D. Albert Fish

16. This unidentified serial killer from the late 1880's who operated in or near the Whitechapel district of London murdered at least 5 female prostitutes and mutilated their bodies in a manner that indicated he had a substantial knowledge of the human anatomy. The case remains London's most famous unsolved mystery.

    A. Jack the Ripper   B. Angel of Death

    C. Torture Doctor   D. Yorkshire Ripper

17. What is America's greatest unsolved killing case in which the serial killer terrorized northern California in the 1960's and 70's, who taunted law enforcement with coded messages?

    A. Green River Killer   B. Backpack Killer

    C. ABC Murderer   D. Zodiac Killer

18. He was a serial killer known as the "Milwaukee Cannibal," who between the years 1978 – 1991 murdered 17 males who he had lured to his home promising sex or money. His crimes included cannibalsim and necrophilia.

    A. Dean Coril   B. Lucian Staniak

    C. Jeffrey Dahmer   D. Wayne Williams

19. Serial killer and rapist, he was one of America's most notorious criminals of the late 20th century. His crime spree from the mid to late 1970's where he left a wake of sexually assaulted and murdered women from Washington, Oregon, Colorado, Utah, and Florida. While he confessed to 28 murders some believe the number to be more in the hundreds.

    A. Cleo Green   B. Ted Bundy

    C. Danny Rolling   D. John Collins

20. He was #1 on the FBI's Most Wanted Terrorist list before he was killed by U.S. Navy Seals in Pakistan in 2011.

    A. Agustin Vásquez   B. Osama bin Laden

    C. Khalid Sheikh Mohammed   D. Bradford Bishop

Answers - Chapter 15 – Bad Guys: Gangsters, Presidents Assassins, Serial Killers, & Terrorist

1. C – Al Capone

2. B – John Dillinger

3. A – Bugsy Siegel

4. B – Baby Face Nelson

5. D – Lucky Luciano

6. C – John Gotti

7. A – Pretty Boy Floyd

8. D – Carlo Gambino

9. C – John Wilkes Booth

Did You Know: *While Lincoln was the first president to have been assassinated, to date there have been 4 presidents who have suffered the same fate: Abraham Lincoln, James Garfield, William McKinley, and John F. Kennedy. There have been attempts made on several other of the presidents: William H. Taft, Theodore Roosevelt, Herbert Hoover, two attempts made on the life of Franklin D. Roosevelt, 2 attempts made on the life of Harry Truman, an attempt made on Kennedy previous to his assassination, 2 attempts on Richard Nixon, 2 attempts on Gerald Ford, 2 attempts on Jimmy Carter, Ronald Reagan, George H.W. Bush, 4 attempts on Bill Clinton, 2 attempts on George W Bush, and 3 attempts on Barack Obama.*

10. A – Charles Guiteau

11. B – Leon Czolgosz

12. D – Lee Harvey Oswald

Did You Know: *Over 50 years have passed and there are more Americans who believe there is more to this story and a cover-up than there are those who believed the theory that Oswald was the sole shooter and planned this assassination on his own. This is the longest on-going conspiracy theory (other than an alien crashing at*

Roswell, New Mexico) and remains unsolved in most American's eyes as to who was behind the planning of the killing of the president. Some of the accused are: Vice-President Lyndon B. Johnson (who made sure he was sworn in as the next president while on board Air Force One while returning to Washington just 2 hours and 39 minutes after the president had been shot with First Lady Jacqueline Kennedy by his side in her blood-soaked suit), George W. Bush, the CIA, the Russians, Fidel Castro, and the Mafia. Fifty-five years later many of the FBI files on the assassination remain redacted even though the time period the files are normally opened have passed.

13. A – Boston Strangler

14. C – Danny Rolling

15. B – David Berkowitz

16. A – Jack the Ripper

17. D – Zodiac Killer

18. C – Jeffrey Dahmer

19. B – Ted Bundy

20. B – Osama bin Laden

16

Men of Science

Answers for this chapter on page 127

1. He was a Scottish physician, microbiologist, and pharmocologist who discovered penicillin.

    A. Frederick Banting   B. Frederick Chapman Robbins

    C. Alexander Fleming   D. Herman Koch

2. He is considered the most influential physicist of the 20th Century. He developed the general theory of relativity.

    A. Nikola Tesla   B. Albert Einstein

    C. Stephen Hawking   D. Isaac Newton

3. He began the scientific revolution publishing his evidence that Earth orbits the sun.

    A. Carl Sagan   B. Galileo Galilei

    C. Nicolaus Copernicus   D. Johannes Kepler

4. Though he is most remembered for the annual prizes given out

annually in his name for science, literature, and peace; he invented (and manufactured) dynamite, the blasting cap, gelignite, and ballistite.

    A. Alfred Nobel   B. Benjamin Franklin

    C. Dan David Prize   D. Albert Einstein

5. An American astronomer, he is regarded as one of the most important astronomers of all time. His research helped prove that the universe is expanding and he created a classification system for galaxies that has been used for decades.

    A. Archimedes   B. Edwin Hubble

    C. Robert Hooke   D. Josef Allen Hynek

6. A Greek physician who lived during the Age of Pericles, he is the founder of medicine as a science. He is known to have made this statement, "Let food be thy medicine and medicine be thy food."

    A. Galen   B. Ibn Sina / Avicenna

    C. Joseph Lister   D. Hippocrates

7. He is regarded as the 'Father of Paleontology.'

    A. George Cuvier   B. Jack Horner

    C. Mark Loewen   D. Alan Grant

8. Italian astronomer who was one of the most significant people in the history of science. He is considered the "Father of Modern Science," who made pioneering observations laying the foundation for modern physics and astronomy.

    A. Arthur Eddington   B. Giovanni Cassini

  C. Galileo Galileo   D. Joseph Louis Lagrange

9. A German physicist who is best-known for his role as the originator of quantum theory.

  A. Max Planck   B. Werner Heisenberg

  C. J. Robert Oppenheimer   D. Klaus Fuchs

10. English astronomer who was the first to calculate the orbit of a comet, which was later named after him.

  A. Nicolaus Copernicus   B. Edmond Halley

  C. Johannes Kepler   D. Antony Hewish

11. He is perhaps the greatest physicist who has ever lived (along with Albert Einstein, who is also a contender for the title). He is most famous for his law of gravitation. You most likely learned about him through the story of him sitting under the tree and an apple fell hitting him on the head giving him insight into how gravity works.

  A. Archimedes   B. Michael Faraday

  C. Max Planck   D. Isaac Newton

12. He was the Swedish astronomer who invented the Celsius, or centigrade, thermometer scale.

  A. Johannes Kepler   B. Christopher Wren

  C. Anders Celsius   D. William Herschel

13. He was one of the greatest inspirations to modern science. He established the school *The Lyceum*, making big contributions to science

education which changed the way students thought about different areas of physical sciences. He taught reasoning, observation, and examination. His method is similar to what is used in science experiments in labs today.

    A. Aristotle   B. Archimedes

    C. Galileo Galilei   D. Louis Pasteur

14. German astronomer and astrologer best known for his laws of planetary motion.

    A. Joseph LeGrange   B. Galileo Galilei

    C. Johannes Kepler   D. Nicolaus Copernicus

15. African-American agricultural chemist who discovered 300 uses for peanuts and hundreds more for soybeans, pecans, and sweet potatoes.

    A. Percy Lavon Julian   B. Benjamin Bannecker

    C. Charles Drew   D. George Washington Carver

16. He is the founder of genetics and identified many of the rules of heredity.

    A. James Watson   B. Thomas Morgan

    C. Gregor Mendel   D. Norman Borlaug

17. This Austrian American immunologist and pathologist received the 1930 Nobel Prize for Physiology or Medicine for his discovery of the major blood groups and blood typing.

    A. David Baltimore   B. Karl Landsteiner

    C. John Franklin Enders   D. Jules Bordet

18. He was the founder of modern microbiology.

    A. Louis Pasteur   B. Michael Faraday

    C. Jonas Salk   D. Craig Brackett

19. An English physician who was the first to recognize the full circulation of the blood.

    A. William Harvey   B. Robert Quigley

    C. Benjamin Spock   D. William Harvey

20. This American physician developed the first effective polio vaccine.

    A. Edward Jenner   B. Rene Laennec

    C. Jonas Salk   D. Henry Gray

21. He is often cited as the greatest biologist in history due to his famous work, 'On The Origin Of Species,' which explains the theory of evolution by natural selection.

    A. Richard Dawkins   B. Charles Darwin

    C. Carl Linnaeus   D. Alfred Kinsey

22. 'Father of Nuclear Chemistry,' this German chemist discovered the radiochemical proof of nuclear fission.

    A. Nikola Tesla   B. Otto Wallach

    C. Konrad Bloch   D. Otto Hahn

23. American theoretical physicist and director of the Los Alamos

Laboratory during the Manhattan Project who was responsible for research and design of the atomic bomb. He is often called the 'Father of the Atomic Bomb.'

    A. Edward Teller   B. Albert Einstein

    C. Robert Oppenheimer   D. Klaus Fuchs

24. Nicknamed 'Einstein' as a schoolboy, this British scientist and physicist was known for his groundbreaking work with black holes and relativity. He wrote 'A Brief History of Time,' which was an international bestseller. He also wrote science adventure books for children. At the age of 21 he was diagnosed with ALS. He passed away in 2018, his ashes were buried at Westminster Abbey, and his recorded voice was beamed into space to the nearest black hole.

    A. Chuck Hailey   B. Stephen Hawking

    C. John Michell   D. John Wheeler

25. This Austrian is the founding father of psychoanalysis.

    A. Alois Alzheime   B. Roger Bannister

    C. Carl Jung   D. Sigmund Freud

Answers - Chapter 16 – Men Of Science

1. C – Alexander Fleming

2. B – Albert Einstein

Did You Know: *He was a German physicist who immigrated to the U.S. after being targeted by the Nazis. His work had a major impact on the development of atomic energy.*

3. C – Nicolaus Copernicus

4. A – Alfred Nobel

5. B – Edwin Hubble

6. D – Hippocrates

7. A – Georges Cuvier

Did You Know: *He ruled out evolution as a mechanism for producing new species, believing they followed naturally after catastrophes.*

8. C – Galileo Galileo

9. A – Max Planck

10. B – Edmond Halley

11. D – Isaac Newton

12. C – Anders Celsius

13. A – Aristotle

14. C – Johannes Kepler

15. D – George Washington Carver

16. C – Gregor Mendel

17. B – Karl Landsteiner

18. A – Louis Pasteur

Did You Know: *He was one of three of the main founders of microbiology with his work on fermentation, his discovery of anaerobic bacteria, and his germ theory of disease. This French chemist and microbiologist's contributions to science, technology, and medicine are without precedent. He developed vaccines against rabies and anthrax. Pasteurization, the process he invented to stop foodstuffs from going bad is still in use today.*

19. A – William Harvey

20. C – Jonas Salk

21. B – Charles Darwin

22. D – Otto Hahn

23. C – Robert Oppenheimer

24. B – Stephen Hawking

25. D – Sigmund Freud

17

Inventors

Answers for this chapter on page 137

1. He is described as America's greatest inventor and one of the most famous men in the world. He held more than 1,000 patents for his inventions. To name just a few: incandescent electric light bulb, phonograph, telegraph, and one of the earliest motion picture cameras.

    A. Benjamin Franklin   B. James Watt

    C. Samuel Morse   D. Thomas Edison

2. In 1593 he noticed how the density of a liquid changes with temperature and he invented the thermometer.

    A. Galileo Galilei   B. Blaise Pascal

    C. Anders Celsius   D. Gabriel Fahrenheit

3. Around the year 105 A.D. he made the first paper in China.

    A. Su Song   B. Cai Lun

    C. Jackie Chan   D. Bruce Lee

4. This French Benedictine monk was making wine and couldn't get rid of the bubbles. When he tasted his accidental concoction he declared he was "drinking the stars." This is the legend of how this monk created champagne.

    A. T'sai lun   B. Matthieu Ricard

    C. Dom Pérignon   D. Brother Marie Paques

5. It was during the Middle Ages that he invented the first printing press with movable type in the year 1450.

    A. Johanna Drucker   B. Johannes Gutenberg

    C. George Phineas Gordon   D. Valentin Bapst

6. Coca-cola, the soft drink was invented in a brass kettle in the backyard of this doctor in Atlanta, Georgia in 1886.

    A. John Pemberton   B. Ted Turner

    C. Charles Elmer Hires   D. Caleb Bradham

7. It was the early 19th century in the year 1800 when this Italian made the first battery.

    A. André-Marie Ampère   B. Allessandro Volta

    C. Georg Ohm   D. Luigi Galvani

8. In the 1830's what Frenchman invented a method or process of taking photographs? He became known as one of the fathers of photography.

    A. Henri Cartier-Bresson   B. Alfred Stieglitz

    C. Lewis Hine   D. Louis Daguerre

9. This American inventor is best remembered for his invention of the single-wire telegraph system and co-inventor of the code used for communication with the wire which was named for him.

    A. Thomas Edison   B. John Logie Baird

    C. Samuel Morse   D. Herman Hollerith

10. This German invented the gasoline powered automobile.

    A. Henry Ford   B. Nicolas Joseph Cugnot

    C. Wilhelm Maybach   D. Karl Benz

11. This Scottish engineer was one of the inventors of the mechanical television and the first color television system. He was the first man to televise pictures of objects in motion.

    A. John Baird   B. Philco Farnsworth

    C. Boris Rosing   D. Guglielmo Marconi

12. These two brothers built the first engine-powered airplane in 1903.

    A. the Montgolfier brothers   B. the Duryea brothers

    C. the Wright brothers   D. the Jacuzzi brothers

13. A Serbian (what is Croatia today) American inventor, he was one of the most innovative and mysterious men who ever lived. He invented the first alternating current (AC) motor and developed AC generation and transmission technology. The AC systems he championed and improved remains the global standard for power transmission.

    A. Thomas Edison   B. Nikola Tesla

    C. Martin Eberhard   D. Elon Musk

14. This Dutch-German-Polish physicist and maker of scientific instruments is best known for inventing the first mercury thermometer.

    A. Leon Battista Alberti   B. Evangelista Torricelli

    C. Anders Celsius   D. Gabriel Fahrenheit

15. It was an Italian inventor who developed, demonstrated, and marketed the first successful long-distance wireless telegraph.

    A. Guglielmo Marconi   B. Leonardo da Vinci

    C. Jean Foucault   D. Galileo Galilei

16. This American inventor and Founding Father invented the lightening rod, bifocals, a stove named for him, and the glass harmonica.

    A. Michael Faraday   B. Robert Goddard

    C. Lewis Waterman   D. Benjamin Franklin

17. A friend of Benjamin Franklin who was also an inventor and a chemist invented carbonated or soda water, laughing gas, and co-discoverer of oxygen.

    A. Earle Dickson   B. Joseph Priestly

    C. Dean Kamen   D. Richard Drew

18. He was the inventor of the cotton gin and a pioneer in the mass production of cotton due to his invention.

    A. Eli Whitney   B. Thomas Sullivan

    C. George Washington Carver   D. Alexander Fleming

19. He is best known for his invention of the telephone.

    A. Elisha Gray   B. Gardiner Greene Hubbard

    C. Alexander Graham Bell   D. Joseph Henry

20. A Swedish engineer and industrialist is the one who gave us the ability to blow holes in mountains enabling us to make roads and to blow things up with his invention of dynamite. It was his construction work that inspired him to find ways of blasting rock.

    A. Tom Blake   B. Alfred Nobel

    C. Eugene Figg   D. Gutzon Borglum

21. He made the first motorcycle with a gasoline engine.

    A. Gottlieb Daimler   B. William S. Harley

    C. Max Fritz   D. James Lansdowne Norton

22. It was 1902 when he invented the air conditioner.

    A. Joseph Gayetty   B. Cyrus McCormick

    C. Willis Carrier   D. Philip Diehl

23. Fresh fruits and vegetables available year round along with ready made frozen food is possible thanks to this American taxidermist.

    A. Oliver Evans   B. Nicolas Appert

    C. Eli Whitney   D. Clarence Birdseye

24. There isn't a child in America, or probably the world, who most

likely hasn't enjoyed the invention of these two men. These cousins invented the Crayola brand crayons.

    A. Wrights   B. Braun & Farnsworth

    C. Binney & Smith   D. Otis

25. *There are 2 correct answers.* He was a co-inventor who invented the Aqualung for scubadivers?

    A. Emile Gagnan   B. Jacques Cousteau

    C. Richard Branson   D. L. Bruce Jones

26. This South African is an inventor, engineer, and innovator who is the founder and CEO of *SpaceX* and *Tesla Motors* – but he's not done yet. He holds some very futuristic ideas.

    A. Chuck Hull   B. Felix Leiter

    C. Elon Musk   D. Steve Perlman

27. He was the inventor of the reading and writing system named after him which is used by the blind and visually impaired.

    A. Louis Braille   B. James Gale

    C. William Moon   D. Ralph Teetor

28. He was the inventor of the microwave oven.

    A. James Harrison   B. Benjamin Franklin

    C. William Hadaway   D. Percy Spencer

29. This British merchant is given credit for receiving the first patent for the idea of preserving food using tin cans.

    A. Clarence Birdseye   B. Peter Durand

    C. Roy Plunkett   D. Nathaniel C Briggs

30. This African-American inventor is best known for his invention of the gas mask and he also invented the first automatic traffic signal.

    A. Garrett Morgan   B. Elijah McCoy

    C. Lewis Latimer   D. George Washington Carver

31. He is best known for his invention of the barometer.

    A. David C. Collins   B. Evangelista Torricelli

    C. Garrett Augustus Morgan D. Clément Ader

32. In 1927 he invented a powdered drink mix called Kool-Aid.

    A. Edwin Perkins   B. Manoj Bhargava

    C. Torbern Bergman   D. Peter Cooper

33. This computer scientist is best known for his invention of the World Wide Web.

    A. Charles Babbage   B. John Mauchly

    C. Adam Osbourne   D. Tim Berners-Lee

34. These two French brothers made the first practical hot-air balloon.

    A. Pasteur   B. Lassimonne

C. Montgolfier   D. Cassagnes

35. Any of you who have ever been to an ice-hockey game or ice skating event are familiar with the invention of the machine named after it's inventor which comes out to resurface the ice in the ice rink.

    A. John Joseph Merlin   B. Levi Strauss

    C. Whitcomb L. Judson   D. Frank Zamboni

Answers - Chapter 17 – Inventors

1. D – Thomas Edison

2. A – Galileo Galilei

Did You Know: *A few years after inventing the thermometer he built a telescope and made new astronomical discoveries.*

3. B – Cai Lun

Did You Know: *Egyptians around 2500 B.C. produced papyrus, an early version of paper.*

4. C - Dom Pérignon

5. B – Johannes Gutenberg

Did You Know: *Even though Gutenberg is given credit with inventing the first movable printing press, in actuality around 400 years earlier during the Northern Song Dynasty, a Chinese by the name of Bi Sheng gave us the technology for the first movable type printing press.*

6. A – John Pemberton

Did You Know: *It was the doctor's bookkeeper Frank Robinson who suggested what to name the soft drink which was marketed as a tonic made of cocaine and kola. It was also Robinson who scripted the name of Coca-Cola into the logo that has stayed the same since it's inception. The first year of it's invention about 9 servings of the soft drink were sold in a day bringing in $50 for the year.*

7. B – Alessandro Volta

8. D – Louis Daguerre

9. C – Samuel Morse

10. D – Karl Benz

11. A – John Baird

12. C – The Wright brothers (Wilbur & Orville Wright)

13. B – Nikola Tesla

14. D – Gabriel Fahrenheit

15. A – Guglielmo Marconi

Did You Know: In 1901 Marconi broadcast the first transatlantic radio signal. Marconi's radios saved hundreds of lives – including those who survived the sinking of the 'Titanic'. When the 'Titanic' hit the iceberg in 1913, the Marconi operator was able to send out a distress call heard by the 'Carpathia' who was able to save 700 survivors.

16. D – Benjamin Franklin

17. B – Joseph Priestly

18. A – Eli Whitney

19. C – Alexander Graham Bell

Did You Know: He is credited with the invention of the telephone despite hundreds of lawsuits challenging his claim to the invention. He faced a 20-year legal battle with other inventors laying claim that they were the ones who invented the telephone – the most persistent of these being Elisha Grey. However, none of the lawsuits against him were successful.

20. B – Alfred Nobel

21. A – Gottlieb Daimler

22. C- Willis Carrier

23. D – Clarence Birdseye

Did You Know: In attempting to find a way to feed his family food year round that may not be available due to winter weather or being out of season, the idea for this discovery came to him while in the Arctic and observing the Inuit and how they preserved fish by placing them in barrels of sea water that quickly froze. When the fish was later cooked it tasted fresh. He came to the conclusion that the quick freezing retained the food's freshness.

24. C – Binney & Smith

25. Either A or B would be correct. A – Emile Gagnon or B – Jacques

Cousteau

26. C – Elon Musk

27. A – Louis Braille

28. D – Percy Spencer

29. B – Peter Durand

30. A – Garrett Morgan

31. B – Evangelista Torricelli

32. A – Edwin Perkins

Did You Know: *Kool-Aid was initally called "Fruit Smack." It was a rags to riches story for it's creator Edwin Perkins who literally went from living in a sodhouse to a mansion and even survived the Great Depression due to his invention of the sugary drink. In 1900 the family ran a general store where Jell-o was sold which influenced him into creating powdered mix flavored drinks. He experimented in his mother's kitchen until he came up with the winning combination.*

33. D – Tim Berners-Lee

34. C – Montgolfier

35. D – Frank Zamboni

18

Artists

Answers for this chapter on page 150

1. He was a Spanish expatriate and was one of the most influential and most famous artists of the 20th century and co-creator of Cubism. His most well-known Surrealist painting, deemed one of the greatest paintings of all time, completed in 1937 during the Spanish Civil War is the painting *'Guernica,'* which is regarded by many art critics as one of the most moving and powerful anti-war paintings in history.

    A. Pablo Picasso   B. El Greco

    C. Francisco Goya   D. Edgar Degas

2. This 17th century Dutch artist is considered one of the greatest painters and most revered in European history. He's known for his Biblical scenes such as: *'The Storm On The Sea Of Galilee'* and for his self portraits.

    A. Leonardo da Vinci   B. Rembrandt

    C. Sandro Boticelli   D. Caravaggio

3. The name he's known by is a nickname in reference to his Greek origin. He painted many religious works. Landscape paintings were rare in Spanish art at the time and his work *'View of Toledo'* is one of three of his surviving landscapes, and is one of his most cherished masterpieces.

A. El Greco   B. Auguste Rodin

C. Francisco Goya   D. Titian

4. He is a famous French painter and one of the founders of the Impressionism movement. The last 30 some years of his life he painted from his home and gardens in Giverny, France including his series on 'Water Lilies.'

A. Paul Cézanne   B. Edgar Degas

C. Jean-François Millet   D. Claude Monet

5. An American painter who is widely considered one of America's foremost portrait artists. One of his paintings is of George Washington in his last year as president.

A. Emanuel Leutze   B. J.M.W. Turner

C. Gilbert Stuart   D. John Singer Sargent

6. This Italian-born American artist was the most successful portrait painter of his era (late 1800's – early 1900's). His most controversial works, which is now considered one of his best, is 'Portrait of Madame X.' He painted nearly 900 oil paintings, over 2,000 watercolors, sketches, and drawings.

A. Peter Paul Rubens   B. John Singer Sargent

C. Andy Warhol   D. Andrew Wyeth

7. A Dutch painter whose inspirations came from what was familiar to him, mostly from the Delft in the Netherlands where he grew up. In most of his paintings he focused on realistic subjects. Some of his masterpieces were: 'The Girl With the Pearl Earring,' 'The Kitchen Maids,' and 'The Lace Maker.'

A, Pieter Bruegel the Elder   B. Edvard Munch

C. Johannes Vermeer   D. Peter Paul Rubens

8. He is regarded as the greatest German Renaissance artist. His works include religious works, portraits, and self-portraits, woodcuts, and engravings. His 'Self-Portrait at Twenty-Eight' and 'The Four Apostles,' an oil on two wood panels are well-known works by this German artist.

    A. Frederic Remington   B. Gian Lorenzo Bernini

    C. Titian   D. Albrecht Dürer

9. He is the most significant artist of Dutch and Flemish Renaissance painting of the 16th century. His landscapes of the Low Countries and peasant life are easily recognizable as his works. He was head of a painting dynasty which included his two sons. You may be familiar with his paintings, 'Peasant Wedding,' 'The Hunters In The Snow,' or 'Portrait Of An Old Woman.'

    A. Emanuel Leutze   B. Pieter Bruegel the Elder

    C. Hans Holbein the Younger   D. Caravaggio

10. This Norwegian painter of the late 20th century is most well-known for his work titled 'The Scream.'

    A. Edvard Munch   B. J.M.W. Turner

    C. Peter Paul Rubens   D. Auguste Rodin

11. He was the French sculptor best known for designing and executing the Statue of Liberty.

    A. Auguste Rodin   B. Lorenzo Bartolini

    C. Frédéric Auguste Bartholdi   D. Benvenuto Cellini

12. He was one of the best-known American artists of the mid-20th century. His favorite subjects to paint were the land and the people close to him. In 1976, he became the first American artist while still alive to have his work showcased in a big retrospective at the Metropolitan Museum of Art. He was awarded the Presidential Medal of Freedom in 1963 and was the first artist to receive the Congressional Gold Medal in 1990.

    A. Andy Warhol   B. Andrew Wyeth

    C. John Singer Sargent   D. Charles Wilson Peale

13. He was an American artist who spent most of his time in London. He was highly influential in the late 19th century. He won considerable success in Paris with his painting 'Symphony In White, No. 1: The White Girl,' but his most famous works which always comes to mind with this artist is his 'Arrangement in Grey & Black: The Artist's Mother,' better known to the world by his name along with his mother, which is one of the most famous artworks in existence.

    A. Frederic Remington   B. Hokusai

    C. Sandro Boticelli   D. James Whistler

14. He was an American artist best remembered for his portrait paintings of leading figures of the American Revolution.

    A. Charles Wilson Peale   B. Gilbert Stuart

    C. Francisco Goya   D. Henri Matisse

15. A French painter and one of the founders of the Barbizon School (in rural France) who is known for his peasant subjects. Some of his works are: 'The Sower,' 'The Gleaners,' and 'The Angelus.'

    A. Diego Velázquez   B. Henri Matisse

    C. Jean-François Millet   D. Paul Cézanne

16. A 19th century French painter who was one of the first of his century to paint modern life. His last work was 'A Bar at the Folies-Bergère.' Perhaps his most recognizable to the novice, not by name but by sight, is his 'Berthe Morisot With a Bouquet of Violets.'

    A. Pierre-Auguste Renoir   B. Caravaggio

    C. Auguste Rodin   D. Édouard Manet

17. By the 1780's he was Spain's leading artist whose specialty was in religious art and portraits. He was called the 'Father of Modern Art.' He said, "The object of my work is to report the actuality of events," and he did so, which can be seen in his most famous painting, 'The Third of May 1808.'

    A. Edvard Munch   B. Jackson Pollock

    C. Francisco Goya   D. Pablo Picasso

18. He is widely regarded as the most famous artist of the Italian Renaissance and most well-known today for his painting of the ceiling of the Sistine Chapel. Not only an artist but a sculptor, his works 'Pieta,' a sculpture of Mary holding the dead Jesus across her lap and 'David,' the most famous statue in the world are equally impressive works of his.

    A. Raphael   B. Michelangelo

    C. Gian Lorenzo Bernini   D. Titian

19. This Dutch artist is one of the most well-known Post-Impressionist artists whose colors in his works make them easily identifiable as his. The most famous is 'The Potato Eaters,' but 'Irises,' 'Sunflowers,' and 'The Starry Night' are recognizable to even the most novice art lover.

    A. Vincent Van Gogh   B. Leonardo da Vinci

    C. Titian   D. Auguste Rodin

20. A French Post-Impressionist painter he found his own style when he incorporated vivid colors into his artwork realizing painting should be done from nature. He painted over 900 oils and 400 watercolors and is best known for his varied painting styles paving the way for the emergence of 20th century modernism. There were three subjects repeatedly seen in his art: Mont St. Victorie, bathers, and still lifes which included apples.

    A. Diego Velázquez   B. Johannes Vermeer

    C. Paul Cézanne   D. Albrecht Dürer

21. This French sculptor's work had a huge influence on modern art. A fateful trip to Italy where he was inspired and awakened to new possibilities after seeing Michelangelo's works he went on to sculpt great pieces such as: 'The Vanquished,' 'The Thinker,' and 'The Kiss.'

    A. Auguste Rodin   B. Leonardo da Vinci

    C. Frédéric Auguste Bartholdi   D. Lorenzo Bartolini

22. An American artist who was a leading figure of Pop art. He was one of the most popular artists of his time. His style was both avant-garde and commercial. His 'Campbell's Soup Cans' is his signature piece.

    A. Hokusai   B. James Whistler

    C. El Greco   D. Andy Warhol

23. An Italian painter and the supreme painter of the High Renaissance; he was one of the trinity of High Renaissance painters (which also included Michaelangelo and Leonardo da Vinci). He is best known for his Madonnas and for his figures at the Palace at the Vatican.

    A. Raphael   B. Gian Lorenzo Bernini

    C. Titian   D. Sandro Botticelli

24. An Italian painter of the Early Renaissance, he worked under the patronage of Lorenzo de' Medici. One of the greatest painters of the Florentine Renaissance, he painted many devotional paintings. Some of his works are: 'The Birth of Venus,' 'Adoration Of The Magi,' and 'Venus & Mars.'

    A. Emanuel Leutze   B. Caravaggio

    C. Sandro Botticelli   D. Leonardo da Vinci

25. This Italian was probably the most revolutionary artist of his time – from the early 1590's through 1610. Rules that had guided artists for a century he abandoned and almost single-handedly created the Baroque style. His first major piece was 'The Fortune Teller,' while his first masterpiece was 'The Cardsharps.' Many of his paintings dealt with death, such as: 'The Crucifixion of Saint Peter,' 'The Decapitation of Saint John the Baptist,' and 'The Entombment.'

    A. Johannes Vermeer   B. Vinvent Van Gogh

    C. Gian Lorenzo Bernini   D. Caravaggio

26. He was a French artist who was active during the end of the 19th century and early 20th century. He was among the leading painters of the art movement Impressionism. Most known for his paintings of women and Parisian society, he used vibrant colors and loose brushwork. Some of his most recognizable works are: 'Bal du Moulin de la Galette,' 'Luncheon At The Boating Party,' 'The Umbrellas,' and 'Two Sisters (On The Terrace).'

    A. Edgar Degas   B. Pierre-Auguste Renoir

    C. Albrecht Dürer   D. Henri Matisse

27. A Flemish (Belgian) artist who is considered the most influential artist of Flemish Baroque tradition. His subjects varied from religious, mythology, and historical. He is credited with over 1,000 works. Some of his best work includes: 'Samson & Delilah,' 'The Descent From The Cross,' and 'A View Of Het Steen In the Early Morning,' a landscape many art critics rate as

one of the best landscapes of the Baroque era.

    A. Peter Paul Rubens   B. Pieter Bruegel the Elder

    C. Johannes Vermeer   D. Hans Holbein the Younger

28. An American painter, illustrator, and sculptor who specialized in depictions of the American Old West. He completed more than 70 paintings, though it is his bronze statues, among the best of American sculpture that he is most famous for. 'The Bronco Buster' is probably the most well-known of his sculptures.

    A. J.M.W. Turner   B. Frederic Remington

    C. Jasper Johns   D. Alexander Calder

29. A French artist that painted many subjects, more than half of which depict dancers. He was one of a group of painters who came to be known as the Impressionists, though he preferred the term Realists. Many when they think of him his paintings of ballerinas come to mind, such as: 'The Star' 'The Dance Class,' and 'Dancers Practicing At The Bar.' Equally impressive works of his are: 'The Absinthe Drinker, 'Place de la Concorde,' and 'A Cotton Office In New Orleans.'

    A. Paul Cézanne   B. Jean-François Millet

    C. Henri Matisse   D. Edgar Degas

30. The greatest Italian Renaissance painter of the Venetian school who even in his lifetime was recognized as a supremely great painter, and his reputation has not diminished over the centuries. He painted a wide range of subjects from landscapes, portraits, to spiritual subjects. In his lifetime he was second only to Michaelangelo. Some of his works include: 'Christ Carrying the Cross,' 'Sacred & Profane Love,' and 'Bacchus & Ariadne.'

    A. Rembrandt   B. Leonardo da Vinci

C. Gian Lorenzo Bernini   D. Titian

31. An American painter who was one of the most famous artists of the 20th century and was the leading force behind the Abstract Expressionist movement in the art world. He developed one of the most radical abstract styles in the history of modern art. He used the drip & splash style, the all-over method of painting. His work is easily identifiable. Some of his works are: 'Mural,' 'Lavender Mist,' 'the Flame,' and 'Number 5.'

    A. Gilbert Stuart   B. Hokusai

    C. Jackson Pollock   D. Andy Warhol

32. A leading artist of the Italian Renaissance of the 15th century, he was not only a painter but an inventor. He is most known for two of his works: 'The Last Supper,' and the world's most famous painting 'Mona Lisa.'

    A. Vincent Van Gogh   B. Leonardo da Vinci

    C. Pierre-Auguste Renoir   D. Auguste Rodin

33. An Italian sculptor he was the leading sculptor of his era who is credited with creating the Baroque style of sculpture. "What Shakespeare is to drama, this man is to sculptue," has been said of him. One of his main works was 'The Rape of Proserpina.'

    A. Gian Lorenzo Bernini   B. Frederic Remington

    C. Peter Paul Rubens   D. Raphael

34. This German American painter is best-known for his painting 'Washington Crossing the Delaware.' While there is hardly an American that doesn't instantly recognize this famous painting, there are few who can name the artist who painted it.

    A. Charles Wilson Peale   B. Gilbert Stuart

C. John Trumbell   D. Emanuel Leutze

35. A German painter who is known for the compelling realisms of his portraits. One portrait that comes to mind is the most famous portrait of King Henry VIII of England.

    A. Pieter Bruegel the Elder   B. Hans Holbien the Younger

    C. Edvard Munch   D. Peter Paul Rubens

Answers - Chapter 18 - Artists

1. A – Pablo Picasso

Did You Know: Guernica, the oldest town of the Basque provinces of Spain was completely destroyed by German aircraft. Spanish government had asked Picasso to paint for their exhibit at the Paris World Exhibition and this was his personal view of the tragedy at Guernica.

2. B – Rembrandt

3. A – El Greco

4. D – Claude Monet

5. C – Gilbert Stuart

6. B – John Singer Sargent

7. C – Johannes Vermeer

8. D – Albrecht Dürer

9. B – Pieter Bruegel the Elder

10. A – Edvard Munch

11. C – Frédéric Auguste Bartholdi

12. B – Andrew Wyeth

13. D – James Whistler

14. A – Charles Wilson Peale

15. C – Jean-François Millet

16. D – Édouard Manet

17. C – Francisco Goya

Did You Know: The painting is a depiction of the people of Madrid rebelling against the occupation of the city by Napoleon's army, in which the painting shows where hundreds of Spaniards were round up and shot. The painting is considered one of the first great paintings of the modern era.

18. B – Michelangelo

Did You Know: *The fresco on the ceiling of the Sistine Chapel took Michelangelo four years to complete. The painting contains over 300 figures covering over 500 square meters (equivalent to 5381.9 square feet) of ceiling depicting scenes from the book of Genesis of the Bible.*

19. A – Vincent Van Gogh

20. C – Paul Cézanne

21. A – Auguste Rodin

22. D – Andy Warhol

23. A – Raphael

24. C – Sandro Botticelli

25. D – Caravaggio

26. B – Pierre-Auguste Renoir

27. A – Peter Paul Rubens

28. B – Frederic Remington

29. D – Edgar Degas

30. D – Titian

31. C – Jackson Pollock

Did You Know: *Pollock's painting 'No. 5' was sold in 1949 for $1,500. Bought by another artist, Alfonso Ossorio, his partner when he saw the painting said, "You spent money on that?" The painting became one of Pollock's most iconic works and was sold in 2006 at auction for $165.4 million, making it one of the ten most expensive paintings sold in history (as of that time); right along with such artists as Cézanne, Picasso, and Van Gogh.*

32. B – Leonardo da Vinci

33. A – Gian Lorenzo Bernini

34. D – Emanuel Leutze

35. B – Hans Holbein the Younger

19

Authors & Poets

Answers for this chapter on page 167

1. He is the most well-known American comic book writer and former editor-in-chief of Marvel Comics. He created Spider-Man, X-Men, the Incredible Hulk, and the Incredible Four.

    A. Frank Miller   B. Stan Lee

    C. Alan Moore   D. Otto Binder

2. He is the legendary author of the 'Iliad' and the 'Odyssey.'

    A. Leo Tolstoy   B. Sun Tzu

    C. Homer   D. Virgil

3. England's national poet and one of the most celebrated authors of all time of British history. He has had more theatrical works performed than any other playwright. He is known as the 'Bard of Avon.'

    A. Nathaniel Hawthorne   B. Lord Byron

    C. Charles Dickens   D. William Shakespeare

4. American author who wrote mostly of the South where he grew up,

including 'The Sound and the Fury,' 'As I Lay Dying,' and 'Absalom, Absalom!'

 A. Robert Lewis Stevenson B. William Faulkner

 C. Edgar Allan Poe D. Truman Capote

5. American writer who wrote the most popular children's books of all time. His most famous works were what many children learned to read with which included memorable characters such as the Cat in the Hat, Horton, and the Grinch.

 A. Dr. Seuss B. A.A. Milne

 C. Lewis Carroll D. Hans Christian Anderson

6. A 19th century French writer who was widely regarded as one of the father's of science fiction is the author of 'Around the World In Eighty Days,' and 'Twenty Thousand Leagues Under The Sea.'

 A. H.G. Wells B. Ray Bradbury

 C. Frank Herbert D. Jules Verne

7. He is the author of 'The Hitchhiker's Guide To The Galaxy.'

 A. Arthur Clarke B. William Gibson

 C. Douglas Adams D. Robert Heinlein

8. He is believed to be the author of 'The Art of War,' which some consider to be the best single book ever written on the subject, which is amazing considering it was written about 2,000 years ago.

 A. Leo Tolstoy B. Sun Tzu

 C. Stephen Ambrose D. Herodotus

9. Scottish author who is considered one of the greatest historical novelists. He is the author of 'Ivanhoe.'

    A. Lord Byron   B. Herman Hesse

    C. Bram Stoker   D. Walter Scott

10. He was an English author best known for his children's stories based on the life of his son and his teddy bear and stuffed animals, which included: a piglet, tiger, pair of kangaroos, and a downtrodden donkey. He was the author of the 'Winnie-the-Pooh' books.

    A. E.B. White   B. A.A. Milne

    C. T.S. Eliot   D. Lewis Carroll

11. American 19th century author who is best known for his book 'The Scarlet Letter,' one of the first mass-produced books in the United States. He also wrote 'The House of the Seven Gables.'

    A. Nathaniel Hawthorne   B. William Faulkner

    C. F. Scott Fitzgerald   D. Ernest Hemingway

12. American writer who wrote the children's books 'Charlotte's Web' and 'Stuart Little.'

    A. E.B. White   B. Brothers Grimm

    C. Rudyard Kipling   D. A.A. Milne

13. One of the greatest British poets and leading figure in the Romantic movement. He wrote the satiric realism of 'Don Juan.'

    A. Miguel de Cervantes   B. Virgil

  C. Lord Byron   D. William Shakespeare

14. A 19th century American Transcendentalist poet. One of his best works is 'Self-Reliance.'

  A. T.S. Eliot   B. Joyce Kilmer

  C. Henry David Thoreau   D. Ralph Waldo Emerson

15. He is considered one of France's greatest Enlightenment writers.

  A. William Butler Yeats   B. Niccolò Machiavelli

  C. Voltaire   D. Virgil

16. Not only was he one of the most well-known statesman of the 20th century, he won the Nobel Prize for Literature in 1953 for his six-volume history of WWII.

  A. John S.D. Eisenhower   B. Winston Churchill

  C. Franklin D. Roosevelt   D. J.D. Salinger

17. He was considered prince of German poets and was one of the most highly gifted and accomplished men of the 18th century. His influence is 2nd only to Martin Luther. Philosophically his influence is indelible. He wrote 'Sturm & Drang.' His writings are described as classical.

  A. Johann Wolfgang von Goethe   B. Geoffrey Chaucer

  C. Homer   D. Virgil

18. A French author of the 19th century who is one of the most highly read French authors. He wrote historical adventure novels including, 'The Three Muskateers,' and 'The Count of Monte Cristo.'

A. Lord Byron   B. William Butler Yeats

C. Machiavelli   D. Alexander Dumas

19. He was the first author to try to make a professional living as a writer. He is considered as the architect of short stories. His Gothic tales are known for their tales of horror, mystery, and macabre. His poem 'The Raven' numbers among the best-known poems in literature.

   A. Joyce Kilmer   B. Oscar Wilde

   C. Edgar Allan Poe   D. Victor Hugo

20. Considered by many to be the greatest novelist of the Victorian era, his works stand out due to creating vivid characters and his depictions of contemporary life. Some of his works are: 'Oliver Twist,' 'A Christmas Carol,' 'David Copperfield,' and 'Great Expectations.'

   A. Charles Dickens   B. J.R.R. Tolkien

   C. F. Scott Fitzgerald   D. Nathaniel Hawthorne

21. An American author who wrote tales of the sea, one of which was 'Moby Dick.'

   A. Ernest Hemingway   B. Jack London

   C. Herman Melville   D. Daniel DeFoe

22. One of America's best and most beloved writers, he wrote the American classics, 'The Adventures of Tom Sawyer,' and 'Adventures of Huckleberry Finn.'

   A. John Steinbeck   B. Mark Twain

   C. Jack London   D. Robert Louis Stevenson

23. An Irish poet and writer whose flamboyant style during the late Victorian era and his homosexuality were the cause for his imprisonment. His novel 'The Picture of Dorian Gray,' considered immoral during the Victorian era is now considered one of his most notable works.

    A. John Steinbeck   B. Boris Pasternak

    C. Bram Stoker   D. Oscar Wilde

24. An American author of the 19th century whose works depict struggles for survival, who was himself a symbol of rugged individualism and always eager for adventure. Those qualities came through in his works, 'White Fang,' and 'Call of the Wild.'

    A. John Steinbeck   B. Jack London

    C. William Faulkner   D. Ernest Hemingway

25. An Irish writer who was the author of 'Ulysses' and 'Finnegan's Wake.'

    A. James Joyce   B. Joyce Kilmer

    C. Walt Whitman   D. Fyodor Dostoersky

26. American poet who wrote the poem 'Trees.'

    A. Henry David Thoreau   B. Ralph Waldo Emerson

    C. Fernando Pessoa   D. Joyce Kilmer

27. An English writer and one of the best-known fantasy writers who wrote 'The Hobbit' and 'The Lord of the Rings' trilogy.

    A. Isaac Asimov   B. Jonathan Swift

    C. J.R.R. Tolkien   D. Jules Verne

28. An American writer of the Jazz Age who is widely regarded as one of the greatest American writers of the 20th century. He was the author of 'The Great Gatsby.'

    A. F. Scott Fitzgerald   B. John Steinbeck

    C. William Faulkner   D. Ernest Hemingway

29. Author of approximately 40 books, many of which are on Christian apologetics. He is best known for his 'Chronicles of Narnia' fantasy series.

    A. Charles Dickens   B. J.R.R. Tolkien

    C. Charles Darwin   D. C.S. Lewis

30. He was an American novelist and short-story writer. After WWI he joined other expatriates in Paris where he wrote his first important work, 'The Sun Also Rises.' He also wrote the story of an ambulance driver during the war (which he had been) which was called 'A Farewell To Arms.' Again writing of personal experiences he wrote 'For Whom The Bell Tolls,' about the civil war in Spain. His most memorable short novel was 'The Old Man and the Sea.'

    A. William Faulkner   B. Ernest Hemingway

    C. Fernando Pessoa   D. Robert louis Stevenson

31. This American author wrote about the economic hardships faced by many during the Great Depression in his book, 'The Grapes Of Wrath.' A few of his other works are: 'Tortilla Flat,' 'Of Mice and Men,' and 'Cannery Row.'

    A. John Steinbeck   B. Jonathan Swife

    C. Nathaniel Hawthorne   D. William Faulkner

32. This English writer wrote 'Animal Farm' and 'Nineteen Eighty-Four.'

    A. Niccolò Machiavelli   B. William Butler Yeats

    C. George Orwell   D. Alexander Dumas

33. British author who wrote children's classics, such as: 'Charlie & The Chocolate Factory,' 'The Giant Peach,' 'Matilda,' and 'The BFG' (Big Friendly Giant).

    A. Dr. Seuss   B. Roald Dahl

    C. Samuel Clemens   D. Douglas Adams

34. This American writer is best-known for his science fiction works. He was one of the 20th century's most prolific writers. He is the author of 'I, Robot,' and the 'Foundation' trilogy.

    A. Jules Verne   B. H.G. Wells

    C. Isaac Asimov   D. Orson Scott Card

35. This Irish poet is widely considered to be one of the greatest poets of the 20th century. His writing drew extensively from sources in Irish mythology and folklore.

    A. William Butler Yeats   B. Lord Byron

    C. Douglas Adams   D. Walt Whitman

36. American poet and essayist who is best-known for his book 'Walden,' a reflection on simple living in natural surroundings.

    A. Nathaniel Hawthorne   B. Geoffrey Chaucer

    C. Ralph Waldo Emerson   D. Henry David Thoreau

37. He was an English naturalist who wrote about his scientific theory of evolution in 'On The Origin Of Species.' More than a decade later he wrote 'The Descent Of Man.'

    A. George Orwell   B. Charles Darwin

    C. Isaac Asimov   D. C.S. Lewis

38. An English-born American political activist and revolutionary, this man authored two of the most influential pamphlets that inspired the Founding Fathers and patriots for the American cause. His writings which influenced the American Revolution were 'Common Sense' and 'The American Crisis.'

    A. Thomas Paine   B. Leo Tolstoy

    C. Nathaniel Hawthorne   D. Lord Byron

39. An Italian writer of the Renaissance period is best-known for writing 'The Prince,' a handbook for unscrupulous politicians.

    A. Geoffrey Chaucer   B. Lord Byron

    C. Fernando Pessoa   D. Niccolò Machiavelli

40. American poet who was considered one of the 20th century's major poets . He is the author of 'The Waste Land,' which is now considered by many to be the most influential poetic work of the 20th century.

    A. Douglas Adams   B. Boris Pasternak

    C. T.S. Eliot   D. Alexander Dumas

41. Russian author who wrote 'Doctor Zhivago,' set in the period from the socialist revolution of 1905 through WWII. The novel was an international bestseller but could only be circulated in secrecy in his

own country.

    A. Leo Tolstoy   B. Boris Pasternak

    C. Roald Dahl   D. Alexander Dumas

42. French author who was the most important of the French Romantic writers. In his country of France he is regarded as one of their country's greatest poets. He is best known for 'Les Miserables' and 'The Hunchback of Notre Dame.'

    A. Victor Hugo   B. Alexander Dumas

    C. Herman Hesse   D. Rudyard Kipling

43. A Spanish writer who is considered one of the most famous figures in Spanish literature. In the early 1600's he created one of the world's greatest literary masterpieces, 'Don Quixote.'

    A. Victor Hugo   B. Miguel de Cervantes

    C. Roald Dahl   D. Daniel DeFoe

44. He is the English writer who wrote 60 mystery stories featuring the detective Sherlock Holmes and his assistant Watson.

    A. Oscar Wilde   B. James Joyce

    C. Victor Hugo   D. Arthur Conan Doyle

45. British author who is best-known for his science fiction novels. Some of his well-known works are: 'The Time Machine,' 'The War Of The Worlds,' and 'The Invisible Man.'

    A. H.G. Wells   B. Ray Bradbury

    C. Isaac Asimov   D. Hugo Gernsback

46. Russian author who is regarded as one of the greatest authors of all time. He wrote 'War and Peace,' 'Anna Karenina,' and 'The Death of Ivan Ilyich.'

    A. Roald Dahl   B. Leo Tolstoy

    C. Boris Pasternak   D. Jonathan Swift

47. British author who wrote 'Alice's Adventures In Wonderland' and it's sequel 'Through The Looking Glass and What Alice Found There.' In 1932, 60 some years after he wrote 'Alice's Adventures In Wonderland,' it was one of the most popular children's books in the world and to this day remains a favorite.

    A. Brothers Grimm   B. Hans Christian Anderson

    C. A. Milne   D. Lewis Carroll

48. A 19th century Scottish writer who is best-known for writing 'Treasure Island,' 'Kidnapped,' and 'Strange Case of Dr. Jekyll and Mr. Hyde.'

    A. Walter Scott   B. Robert Louis Stevenson

    C. Daniel DeFoe   D. Herman Melville

49. Jacob & Wilhelm, were two German brothers who during the 19th century collected folklore. They were not only authors and publishers, but they were among the most important German scholars of their time. They published the collection of 200 fairy tales. They didn't write them which many believe, but collected the stories. Some of the stories were hundreds of years old already by the time they added them to their collection. Up to this time the stories had been passed on only by oral tradition. They put the stories together in book form in order to keep these wonderful stories from disappearing over time. A few of the stories included in their book were: 'Rapunzel', 'Hansel & Gretel', 'Cinderella', and 'Rumpelstiltskin'.

         A. Romulus & Remus   B. Charles & Augustus Dickens

C. Brothers Grimm   D. Hans Andersons

50. An English author who was born in India wrote tales and poems with his settings about his birthplace. He is best-known for his books: 'The Jungle Book' and 'Just So Stories.'

    A. Rudyard Kipling   B. Herman Melville

    C. Herman Hesse   D. J.D. Salinger

51. He was an Irish author best-known for writing *Gulliver's Travels.*

    A. Walter Scott   B. Jonathan Swift

    C. Daniel DeFoe   D. Bram Stoker

52. He is considered to be the greatest English poet of the Middle Ages. He wrote the unfinished work of 'The Canterbury Tales,' which is considered one of the greatest poetic works in English.

    A. Geoffrey Chaucer   B. William Butler Yeats

    C. James Joyce   D. John Gower

53. A Danish author of the 19th century who wrote children's books that are loved as much today as they were when he wrote them in the 1800's. Some of his wonderful fairy tales are: 'The Little Mermaid,' 'The Princess & The Pea,' 'The Ugly Duckling,' and 'The Emperor's New Clothes.'

    A. Charles Kingsley   B. Lewis Carroll

    C. Robert Louis Stevenson   D. Hans Christian Anderson

54. This 20th century American author is famous for his best-seller 'The

Catcher In The Rye.'

    A. Walter Scott   B. J.D. Salinger

    C. Hermann Hesse   D. Oscar Wilde

55. An English writer who initially wrote political pamphlets in the late 1600's. Political opponents repeatedly had him imprisoned for his writing. He took a new literary path in 1719 in his late 50's when he wrote 'Robinson Crusoe,' which is 2nd only to the Bible in it's number of translations.

    A. William Butler Yeats   B. Niccolò Machiavelli

    C. Daniel DeFoe   D. Victor Hugo

56. An American poet who is among the most influential poets, well-known for his verse collection 'Leaves of Grass.'

    A. Walt Whitman   B. James Joyce

    C. William Wordsworth   D. Henry Wadsworth Longfellow

57. Irish author best-known for his Gothic tale 'Dracula.'

    A. Bram Stoker   B. Horace Walpole

    C. Victor Hugo   D. Matthew Lewis

58. An ancient Roman poet who was regarded by the Romans as their greatest poet. He is best known for his national epic, 'The Aeneid.'

    A. Homer   B. Virgil

    C. Grattius   D. Gaius Rabirius

59. He has been described as one of the most significant literary figures of the 20th century and one of the greatest poets in the Portuguese language.

    A. Kirmen Uribe   B. Miguel de Cervantes

    C. Victor Hugo   D. Fernando Pessoa

60. American author chiefly famous for his children's books. He is the author of 'The Wizard of Oz' and wrote 14 books in the Oz series.

    A. P.L. Travers   B. L. Frank Baum

    C. Maurice Sendak   D. Shel Silverstein

Answers - Chapter 19 - Authors & Poets

1. B - Stan Lee

2. C - Homer

3. D - William Shakespeare

4. B - William Faulkner

5. A - Dr. Seuss

6. D - Jules Verne

7. C - Douglas Adams

8 - B - Sun Tzu

9. D - Walter Scott

10. B - A.A. Milne

11. A - Nathaniel Hawthorne

12. A - E.B. White

13. C - Lord Byron

14. D - Ralph Waldo Emerson

15. C - Voltaire

16. B - Winston Churchill

17. A - Goethe

18. D - Alexander Dumas

19. C - Edgar Allan Poe

20. A - Charles Dickens

21. C - Herman Melville

22. B - Mark Twain

23. D – Oscar Wilde

24. B – Jack London

25. A – James Joyce

26. D – Joyce Kilmer

27. C – J.R.R. Tolkien

28. A – F. Scott Fitzgerald

29. D – C.S. Lewis

30. B – Erenest Hemingway

31. A – John Steinbeck

32. C – George Orwell

33. B – Roald Dahl

34. C – Isaac Asimov

35. A – William Butler Yeats

36. D – Henry David Thoreau

37. B – Charles Darwin

38. A – Thomas Paine

39. D – Niccolò Machiavelli

40. T.S. Eliot

41. B – Boris Pasternak

42. A – Victor Hugo

43. B – Miguel de Cervantes

44. D – Arthur Conan Doyle

45. A – H.G. Wells

46. B – Leo Tolstoy

47. D – Lewis Carroll

48. B – Robert Louis Stevenson

49. C – Brothers Grimm

50. A – Rudyard Kipling

51. B – Jonathan Swift

52. A – Geoffrey Chaucer

53. D – Hans Christian Anderson

54. B – J.D. Salinger

55. C – Daniel DeFoe

56. A – Walt Whitman

57. A – Bram Stoker

Did You Know: *'Dracula' was Stoker's masterpiece which had been written in the form of diaries and journals kept by the character Jonathan Harker who first made contact with the vampire. Written in 1897 the novel and the character Dracula remain immensely popular.*

58. B – Virgil

59. D – Fernando Pessoa

60. B – L. Frank Baum

20

Musicians

Answers for this chapter on page 187

1. He was one of the most influential figures in jazz whose career spanned 5 decades. He was a trumpeter, bandleader, singer, soloist, and film star. Nicknamed "Satchmo" and "Pops," his trumpet style and unique vocals made you stand up and take notice. He sings these songs like no other before or after him: 'Hello, Dolly,' "What A Wonderful World,' 'When the Saints Go Marchin' In,' and 'Heebie Jeebies.'

    A. Cab Calloway   B. Louis Armstrong

    C. Frank Zappa   D. Miles Davis

2. The greatest American composer of the 20th century. A composer of opera, jazz, and songs for stage and screen. His best-known work is 'Rhapsody In Blue' which he composed when he was only 25. His American opera 'Porgy & Bess' is still one of the most beloved operas ever written. He died at the age of 38 after having brain surgery to remove a tumor.

    A. Glenn Miller   B. Claude DeBussy

    C. George Gershwin   D. Aaron Copland

3. A Polish composer of the Romantic era who wrote primarily for solo piano. At age 8 he made his first public performance and 3 years later

played for the Russian tsar Alexander I. The folk music of Poland gave inspiration to his work. He wrote the 'Nocturne' and what we all know as the funeral march from one of his sonatas.

  A. Frédéric Chopin   B. Ludwig van Beethoven

  C. Franz Liszt   D. Pyotr Ilyich Tchaikovsky

4. An African American jazz savophonist and composer who was sometimes called "Trane." A 20th century music giant with his brooding saxophone is still one of the most recognizable names in modern jazz. 'Blue Train,' 'Giant Steps,' 'My Favorite Things,' and 'A Love Supreme' are among his finest works.

  A. Cab Calloway   B. John Coltrane

  C. Buddy Guy   D. Dizzy Gillespie

5. An English singer, pianist, and composer with a career that has lasted for 5 decades and still going strong. Easily recognizable by his funky glasses and outlandish costumes, he can also be serious, such as when he played at Lady Di's funeral. Such songs as: 'Rocket Man,' 'Tiny Dancer,' and 'Something About The Way You Look Tonight' will have staying power and appeal to fans for many more decades.

  A. Roy Orbbison   B. Ronnie Van Zant

  C. Barry Gibb   D. Elton John

6. Who was the lead vocalist of the rock band Queen?

  A. John Fogarty   B. Syd Barrett

  C. Freddie Mercury   D. Lindsey Buckingham

7. He died in a plane crash at the age of 22, yet he still has had a lasting

impact in music. When only a teen he once opened for Elvis Presley and had to borrow Elvis' guitar to do so. He has been called "the single most influential creative force in early Rock 'n Roll." He was ranked by 'Rolling Stone' magazine as the 13th of the "100 Greatest Artists of All Time." Songs of his that were big hits were: 'That'll Be The Day' and 'Peggy Sue.'

    A. Ray Charles   B. Buddy Holly

    C. Angus Young   D. Roy Orbbison

8. He stood out wearing all black and dark glasses. His singing had a style of it's own. He was nicknamed "The Caruso of Rock" with such songs as: 'Oh, Pretty Woman,' 'Crying,' and 'A Love So Beautiful.'

    A. Gene Krupa   B. Jimmy Page

    C. Johnny Cash   D. Roy Orbbison

9. He was a German composer of the Romantic era. He is widely considered one of the 19th century's greatest composers and leading musicians. His most famous work was 'A German Requiem.'

    A. Claude DeBussy   B. Johann Sebastian Bach

    C. Johannes Brahms   D. Giuseppe Verdi

10. The Beach Boys were an American rock band that were easily distinguishable by their vocal harmonies and surfing songs. They were one of the most influential bands of the rock era. The band included brothers, a cousin, and a friend. Which member of the band was the songwriter who wrote the hits: 'Good Vibrations,' 'In My Room,' 'Help Me, Rhonda,' and 'I Get Around'?

    A. Jim Morrison   B. Brian Wilson

    C. Jimmy Page   D. Tom Petty

11. A blues artist and singer who was a key influence on artists such as Eric Clapton, Jimi Hendrix, Jeff Beck, and Stevie Ray Vaughn. He was from Louisiana and at 7 years old he made himself a guitar and taught himself how to play. His debut album was 'I Left My Blues In San Francisco.'

    A. Buddy Guy   B. Jimi Hendrix

    C. Jerry Garcia   D. Carlos Santana

12. "The Man In Black" was a singer, guitarist, and songwriter whose music was a mix of country, blues, gospel, and rock. His songs such as: 'Folsom Prison Blues,' 'A Boy Named Sue,' and 'I Walk The Line' along with his deep baritone voice make him easy to identify.

    A. Roy Orbbison   B. Bob Dylan

    C. Johnny Cash   D. Waylon Jennings

13. He's an American composer and lyricist who is widely considered one of the greatest songwriters and one of the most prolific songwriters of the 20th century. Some of the songs he wrote were: 'Blue Skies,' 'Easter Parade,' 'God Bless America,' and 'White Christmas.'

    A. George Gershwin   B. Tommy Dorsey

    C. Glenn Miller   D. Irving Berlin

14. This German composer who also became a conductor, was one of the most celebrated figures of the early Romantic period who wrote 'Overture to A Midsummer Night's Dream.' The character of his music was predominently Victorian and he was a favorite composer of Queen Victoria herself. The 'Wedding March' from 'A Midsummer Night's Dream' was played at the wedding of the Princess Royal.

    A. Wolfgang Amadeus Mozart   B. George Frideric Handel

    C. Felix Mendelssohn   D. Richard Wagner

15. Led Zeppelin was formed by this member of the band who also wrote most of their songs. He is ranked as one of the best metal guitarists and an extraordinarily proficient blues guitarist. Songs immortalized from the group are: 'Stairway To Heaven,' 'Kashmir,' and 'Whole Lotta Love.'

  A. Syd Barrett   B. Jimmy Page

  C. Ronnie Van Zant   D. Gregg Allman

16. He's an American singer, guitarist, and songwriter who is one of the best selling music artists of all time. His songs have influenced other songwriters for decades. Some of his hits are: 'Fire & Rain,' 'Country Road,' 'Something In The Way She Moves,' and 'Carolina In My Mind.'

  A. James Taylor   B. John Denver

  C. Bob Dylan   D. Barry Gibb

17. African American trumpeter and composer who developed the music known as bebop. His cheeks ballooned like a bullfrog when this jazz legend played the trumpet. His best-known works include: 'Oop Bob Sh' Bam,' 'A Night In Tunisia,' and 'Groovin' High.' His trumpet playing influenced every player after him and his music is still a major contributing factor in the development of modern jazz.

  A. Cab Calloway   B. Count Bassie

  C. Dizzy Gillespie   D. Duke Ellington

18. Can you name this English rock & blues guitarist, singer, and songwriter? He is the only 3 time inductee to the Rock & Roll Hall of Fame: as a solo artist, with the Yardbirds, and with the Cream. Some of his greatest works are: 'Layla,' 'Tears In Heaven,' 'Cocaine,' and 'I Shot The Sheriff.'

  A. John Fogarty   B. Eric Clapton

C. Barry Gibb   D. Paul McCartney

19. A child prodigy who became one of the most important and influential French composers of all time. He is most well-known for his work 'Claire de Lune' and 'La Mer.'

    A. Tommy Dorsey   B. Benny Goodman

    C. Franz Liszt   D. Claude Debussy

20. He was one of the founding members of the Grateful Dead, lead guitarists, and vocalist.

    A. Syd Barrett   B. Jerry Garcia

    C. Frank Zappa   D. Gene Simmons

21. AC/DC, an Australian rock band formed in the early 1970's by two brothers playing music the group describes as "a rock and roll band, nothing more, nothing less." Lead guitarist, songwriter, and only remaining original member is known for his duck walk who performs in schoolboy uniforms all while playing his energetic guitar rifts that make the crowds go wild.

    A. Angus Young   B. Jim Morrison

    C. Ronnie Van Zant   D. Mark Farner

22. He was an Austrian composer of the late classical and early Romantic eras. He wrote his first masterpiece at the age of 17, 'Gretchen At The Spinning Wheel.' His well-loved music for the 'Ave Maria' was originally to words from Sir Walter Scott's 'Lady of the Lake.' Today, he is one of the world's most frequently performed composers.

    A. Wolfgang Amadeus Mozart   B. Frédéric Chopin

C. Franz Schubert   D. Pyotr Ilyich Tchaikovsky

23. Spanish born tenor who is one of the most popular tenors of all time. He performed around the world as one of the "Three Tenors." He received a dozen Grammy Awards, a Kennedy Center Honor, the U.S. Presidential Medal of Freedom, and an honorary British knighthood. His motto was, "If I rest, I rust." He performed well into his 60's and was known for his versatility. He performed in Italian, French, German, Spanish, English, and Russian.

    A. Luciano Pavarotti   B. Enrico Caruso

    C. Andrea Bocelli   D. Plácido Domingo

24. This African American jazz trumpeter is among the most influential figures in the history of jazz. He developed the improvisational style that defined his trumpet playing. His album 'Kind Of Blue' is credited as the longest-selling jazz album of all time.

    A. Buddy Guy   B. Miles Davis

    C. Cab Calloway   D. Gene Krupa

25. He was an American big band trombonist and bandleader during the swing era. His music dominated the music charts including, 'Chattanooga Choo-Choo,' 'Tuxedo Junction,' and 'Wishing (Will Make It So).' During WWII he headed the U.S. Army Air Force band playing at air bases to boost the morale of the men and to bring them a little music from home. Flying to Paris to perform a Christmas broadcast his plane never reached France and was never found.

    A. Benny Goodman   B. Tommy Dorsey

    C. Glenn Miller   D. Artie Shaw

26. He was one of the best-selling music artists of all time and one of the

most popular and influential singers of the 20th century. He became not only an award winning singer, but also a film actor. He was called "The Voice," "Ole' Blue Eyes," and "The Sultan of Swoon." He was a member of the Rat Pack. Some of his best songs (and it's hard to narrow them down, there were so many) were: 'New York, New York,' 'My Kind Of Town,' 'My Way,' and 'Strangers In The Night.'

 A. Peter Lawford   B. Dan Martin

 C. Sammy Davis, Jr.   D. Frank Sinatra

27. This American singer songwriter has been an influential figure in music for over half a century. He's best known for his gravel-voice singing songs of social and political issues. Tiring of the protest movement he began writing more personal, introspective songs mellowing out from his earlier days. His songs 'Mr. Tambourine Man,' 'All Along the Watchtower,' and 'Like A Rolling Stone' can give you some insight as to why Johnny Cash once introduced him as "the greatest (song)writer of our time."

 A. Bob Dylan   B. James Taylor

 C. Woody Guthrie   D. Tom Petty

28. He was an Italian opera tenor who crossed over into popular music becoming one of the most commercially successful tenors of all time. He helped expand the popularity of opera worldwide. He was a part of the "Three Tenors." In his last major performance at the opening of the Winter Olympics in Italy in 2006 he performed 'Nessun Dorma.'

 A. Plácido Domingo   B. Andrea Bocelli

 C. Mario Lanza   D. Luciano Pavarotti

29. He was an American singer and actor and one of the most popular entertainers of the mid-20th century. He was part of the Rat Pack and part of a duo with Jerry Lewis – one of the most popular comedy teams in movies. His singing career included unforgettable hits, such as: 'That's

Amore,' 'When You're Smiling,' and 'Everybody Loves Somebody.'

    A. Stan Laurel   B. Dean Martin

    C. Oliver Hardy   D. Frank Sinatra

30. An American trombonist and bandleader in the swing era, he was among the first jazz bands to be broadcast on radio. His theme song was 'I'm Getting Sentimental Over You.' Sinatra was the band's main attraction as their singer for three years. This bandleader played both with brother Jimmy and independently.

    A. Miles Davis   B. Benny Goodman

    C. Tommy Dorsey   D. Glenn Miller

31. He was a German Baroque composer whose work 'Messiah,' is among the most famous oratorios in history.

    A. Giuseppe Verdi   B. George Frideric Handel

    C. Ludwig van Beethoven   D. Johann Sebastian Bach

32. He was an Italian operatic tenor of the early 20th century and one of the first musicians to document his voice on recordings. He was dubbed "the man with the orchid-lined voice." In the beginning of his career he auditioned for Giacomo Puccini who was looking for a leading tenor for 'La Boheme.' When Puccini heard his voice he asked him, "Who sent you to me? God himself?" He was the first recording star in history who sold over a million copies.

    A. Luciano Pavarotti   B. Plácido Domingo

    C. José Carreras   D. Enrico Caruso

33. He was a jazz singer and bandleader who regularly performed at the

Cotton Club in Harlem. A master of scat singing he led one of the most popular big bands from the 1930's – '40's. Some of his most well-known songs are: 'Minnie the Moocher,' 'Hi-Dee-Ho Man,' and 'Are You Hep To That Jive.'

    A. Cab Calloway   B. Gene Krupa

    C. Chuck Berry   D. Count Basie

34. He's an American singer, songwriter whose style is a blend of Southern rock, blues, and traditional country. He is the son and namesake of another famous country singer. He made his stage debut at age 8 and performed at the Grand Ole Opry at age 11. His songs include: 'A Country Boy Can Survive,' 'I'm So Lonesome I Could Cry,' or you may be familiar with his song from ABC's Monday Night Football.

    A. Garth Brooks   B. Waylon Jennings

    C. Tim McGraw   D. Hank Williams, Jr.

35. Rolling Stones are an English rock band that formed in 1962 and in the 1970's were the biggest band in the world. Over the decades they have given more large shows internationally than any other band in the world. Some of their hit songs are: '(I Can't Get No) Satisfaction,' 'You Can't Always Get What You Want,' 'Jumpin' Jack Flash,' 'Ruby Tuesday, and 'Time Is On My Side.' Choose from the list below for one of their lead singers.

    A. Eric Clapton   B. Mick Jagger

    C. Angus Young   D. Jim Morrison

36. He's a country singer and songwriter who mixes country and rock 'n roll who remains one of the top selling music artists of all time. Some of his songs are: 'The Dance,' 'Friends In Low Places,' and 'If Tomorrow Never Comes.'

    A. Garth Brooks   B. Keith Urban

C. Kenny Chesney   D. Randy Travis

37. The Beatles were an English rock band formed in 1960 who are considered the most influential music band in history. They not only made music but movies. The first hit from the "Fab Four" was: 'Love Me Do,' and the hits kept rolling on, such as: 'I Want To Hold Your Hand,' 'A Hard Days Night,' 'Let It Be,' 'Yesterday' and those are just their older hits. Which Beatle was a lead singer and one of the main composers of the Beatles songs? After the Beatles broke up he formed a new group called Wings.

A. Ringo Starr   B. John Lennon

C. George Harrison   D. Paul McCartney

38. This American singer, songwriter, and lead singer of his band that was formed in 1976 was equally successful when he went solo. He had a distinctive voice. His friendship with Bob Dylan led to a collaboration with George Harrison, Roy Orbisson, and Jeff Lynne to form the Traveling Wilburys. He put out a solo album, but continued with the band members of the band he was most recognized with. Hits like: 'American Girl,' 'Free Fallin', and 'Don't Do Me Like That' will live on. He passed away in 2017.

John Fogarty   B. Tom Petty

C. Ronnie Van Zant   D. David Bowie

39. He is the singer, songwriter, and musician known for helping to popularize outlaw country music which is influenced by rock. He formed the Highway Men with Willie Nelson, Johnny Cash, and Kris Kristofferson. He was a musical rebel and at the same time a superstar. He wrote the theme song for the TV series The Dukes of Hazzard. One of his most well-known songs is 'I'm A Ramblin' Man.'

A. Johnny Cash   B. Waylon Jennings

C. Merle Haggard   D. Glen Campbell

40. Who was the lead vocalist and primary songwriter of Credence Clearwater Revival? He wrote the songs, "Bad Moon Rising,' and 'Have you Ever Seen The Rain'.

    A. Eric Clapton   B. Steve Perry

    C. Tom Johnston   D. John Fogarty

41. They were one of the best selling music groups in the 1960's, an American folk rock duo who were part of the social revolution. 'Bridge Over Troubled Waters,' was their masterpiece, but 'Cecelia,' 'Scarborough Fair,' and 'Sounds Of Silence' were also loved by the fans of this duo.

    A. Fripp & Eno   B. Simon & Garfunkel

    C. Righteous Brothers   D. Everly Brothers

42. This Austrian composer was not only one of the greatest composers of the classical period, but one of the greatest of all time. By the age of 3 he was playing the clavichord and gave his first public performance at the age of 5. He wrote 'Don Giovanni and the Marriage of Figaro' and 'The Magic Flute' along with one of the most moving pieces in classical music, 'The Requiem.' He wrote and published over 600 published works, yet he died in poverty at the age of 36.

    A. Franz Peter Schubert   B. Felix Mendelssohn

    C. Frédéric Chopin   D. Wolfgang Amadeus Mozart

43. He is the American pianist, singer, and composer who is credited with developing soul music on a style based on melding gospel, rhythm and blues, and jazz. He lost his sight by the age of 7, but began playing the piano professionally by age 15 when he became an orphan. One of his best songs was 'Hit the Road Jack.'

    A. Stevie Wonder   B. José Feliciano

    C. Ray Charles   D. Ronnie Milsap

44. Who was the original creative force behind the band Pink Floyd who led the band to it's fame? He wrote and sang most of Pink Floyd's early songs, but during the years the drugs he took led to a deteriorating mental health issue.

 A. Syd Barrett   B. Robert Plantagenet

 C. Neil Young   D. Roger Daltry

45. He was an American singer, songwriter, and dancer who was one of the most popular entertainers in the world. Dubbed "King of Pop" his album 'Thriller' was the best selling album in history. While still in his youth he was the lead singer of his family's band and went on to have a record breaking solo career with hits 'Billie Jean' and 'Beat It.'

 A. Prince   B. David Bowie

 C. Michael Jackson   D. Peter Gabriel

46. A Mexican-American musician who along with his band made a name for themselves in the late '60's playing a fusion of rock and Latin American jazz, bringing an entirely new sound to the world. With songs like: 'Oye Como Va,' 'Smoke On The Water,' and 'Black Magic Woman' it's no wonder he sold millions of copies of his albums.

 A. Ricky Martin   B. Carlos Santana

 C. Marc Anthony   D. Ruben Blades

47. This American singer and actor is considered one of the most significant cultural icons of the 20th century. He graduated from high school in 1953 and a year later began his singing career with Sun Records in Memphis, and just two years later he was an international sensation. He ushered in a whole new era of music earning himself the nickname "The King of Rock 'n Roll" or simply "The King." He starred in 33 movies and sold more records than any other artist. His first #1 hit was 'Heartbreak Hotel,' and the hits didn't stop there. 'Blue Suede Shoes,' 'Jailhouse Rock,' and 'Are you Lonesome Tonight' are just a few of his memorable songs.

A. Elvis Presley   B. Chuck Berry

C> Jerry Lee Lewis   D. Little Richard

48. He was an American rock guitarist, singer, and songwriter whose short career only lasted 4 years; even so he is regarded as one of the most influential guitarists and most creative musicians. His songs 'Hey Joe,' 'Purple Haze,' 'The Wind Cries Mary,' and 'Foxy Lady' will all be remembered, but his performance at Woodstock playing his version of 'The Star Spangled Banner' drove the audience wild, securing his name in history.

A. Joe Cocker   B. Richie Havens

C. John Sebastian   D. Jimi Hendrix

49. He was a jazz and big band drummer and bandleader who was known for his flamboyant style. He was the first drummer to record using a bass drum and one of the first (if not *the* first) to use a hi-hat. He was known for his extended solos.

A. Sonny Greer   B. Buddy Rich

C. Gene Krupa   D. Phil Collins

50. The Bee Gees, a trio of brothers, who recorded and sang together for 40 years just have one remaining brother in the group. Who is he? Some of their best songs were: 'Lonely Days' and 'I've Gotta Get A Message To You.' They were known for their three-part harmonies and falsetto.

A. Barry Gibb   B. George Michael

C. Bob Marley   D. Daryl Hall

51. He was a German composer of the Baroque era, regarded as one of the greatest composers of all time. He is revered for his work's musical complexities and stylistic innovations. One of his most popular pieces

was 'Toccata' and 'Fugue in D Minor.'

    A. Ludwig van Beethoven   B. Johann Sebastian Bach

    C. Johannes Brahms   D. George Frideric Handel

52. He was a top selling recording artist on both country and pop charts. He was one of the world's best-known and loved performers. A songwriter and performer easily recognizable in his wire frame glasses and Dutch boy haircut, he often sang of nature. Some of his songs were: 'Leavin' On A Jet Plane,' 'Rocky Mountain High,' and 'Thank God I'm A Country Boy.'

    A. Smokey Robinson   B. John Denver

    C. Steve Winwood   D. Seal

53. He became the first African American performer to host a variety TV series in the mid-1950's. He had a soft baritone voice. He performed in big bands and as a jazz pianist . His music is loved as much today as when he originally performed such tunes as: "Mona Lisa,' 'The Christmas Song,' and 'Unforgettable,' which his famous daughter sang posthumously with her father.

    A. Lenny Kravitz   B. Barry White

    C. Nat King Cole   D. George Benson

54. "The King of Swing" an American jazz musician and bandleader whose band had roots in the southern jazz forms of ragtime and Dixieland. His first #1 hit was 'Moonglow.' He helped break down the color barrier having one of the first integrated bands. His band was the first to play jazz at the famed Carnegie Hall along with Count Basie and Duke Ellington.

    A Benny Goodman   B. Charlie Barnett

    C. Glenn Miller   D. Johnny Long

55. What African American bandleader of a jazz orchestra, pianist, and composer whose career spanned over 50 years is considered one of the greatest jazz composers of all time? This Grammy Award winner made it through the Great Depression when most artists didn't. A radio show and tour aided him through the tough times. One of his most popular songs was, 'It Don't Mean A Thing If It Ain't Got That Swing.'

    A. Cab Calloway   B. Billy Eckstine

    C. Duke Ellington   D. Lucky Millinder

56. He was one of the pioneers of rock and roll and was known as the "Father of Rock & Roll." Not only his music drew the crowds, but he was a real showman. His masterpiece was 'Johnny Be Good,' while other favorites were 'Roll Over Beethoven,' and 'Reelin' & Rockin'.'

    A. Miles Davis   B. Chuck Berry

    C. Marvin Gaye   D. Little Richard

57. Since the band was formed in the late '60's, the Allman Brothers became one of America's single most influential bands. They redefined rock music with their mix of blues, country, and jazz giving their music a Southern voice and mixing it up bringing a new sound to the world defined as Southern Rock. The band was started by two brothers along with Dickie Betts, Berry Oakley, Butch Trucks, and Jaimoe. Duane Allman was killed in a motorcycle accident in 1971 and Oakey died just a year later. The band continued with songs like 'The Whipping Post,' 'Black Hearted Woman,' and 'Jessica,' with the soulful vocals of which original band member who passed away in 2017?

    A. Derek Trucks   B. John Mellencamp

    C. Gregg Allman   D. Bob Seger

58. Lynyrd Skynyrd was an American rock band who popularized the Southern rock genre. Such hits as 'Free Bird,' 'Sweet Home Alabama,' and 'Gimme Back My Bullets' secured their position as one of the most

commercially successful Southern Rock groups of the '70's. Unfortunately, their days were numbered as members of the band died in a plane crash in 1977. Who was the lead singer of the band?

    A. Ronnie Van Zant   B. John Fogarty

    C. Danny Joe Brown   D. Jackson Browne

59. He was a German composer and was one of the most recognized and influential of all composers. He was the predominant musical figure in the transitional period between the Classical and Romantic eras. He was widely regarded as the greatest composer who ever lived. He wrote his third symphony in honor of Napoleon Bonaparte when people saw him as a liberator, but when he crowned himself Emperor the composer's viewpoint of him changed. Some of this composers best works are: 'Symphony #3,' 'Symphony #5,' 'The Ninth Symphony,' and 'Fur Elise.'

    A. George Frideric Handel   B. Ludwig van Beethoven

    C. Franz Peter Schubert   D. Frédéric Chopin

60. This African American is considered one of the greatest bandleaders of all time. The arbiter of big-band swing & fusing blues with jazz gave him a style of his own. His nickname was "King of Swing." His music possessed an infectious rhythmic beat. His song 'Every Day I Have The Blues' brought him commercial success.

    A. Nat King Cole   B. Miles Davis

    C. Count Basie   D. Duke Ellington

Answers - Chapter 20 – Musicians

1. B – Louis Armstrong

2. C – George Gershwin

3. A – Frédéric Chopin

Did You Know: While visitng Paris you can see his grave at the cemetery of Père Lachaise, however his heart was interred at the Church of the Holy Cross in Warsaw.

4. B – John Coltrane

5. D – Elton John

6. C – Freddie Mercury

7. B – Buddy Holly

8. D – Roy Orbisson

9. C – Johannes Brahms

10. B – Brian Wilson

11. A – Buddy Guy

12. C – Johnny Cash

13. D – Irving Berlin

14. C – Felix Mendelssohn

15. B – Jimmy Page

16. A – James Taylor

17. C – Dizzy Gillespie

18. B – Eric Clapton

19. D – Claude Debussy

20. B – Jerry Garcia

21. A – Angus Young

22. C – Franz Schubert

23. D – Plácido Domingo

24. B – Miles Davis

25. C – Glenn Miller

26. D – Frank Sinatra

Did You Know: *A colorful character he was for a time on friendly terms with the Kennedys, until the president canceled a weekend visit to Sinatra's home due to his mob connections. Sinatra later became a Republican receiving the Presidential Medal of Freedom from President Reagan. Sinatra had been married 4 times – to his first wife with whom he had 3 children. He married actresses Ava Gardner and Mia Farrow. His last wife he remained married to until his death who was the ex-wife of comedian Zeppo Marx. His son had been kidnapped from his hotel room at gunpoint, one of the most infamous kidnappings in American history. The ransom was paid and his son was released.*

27. A – Bob Dylan

28. D – Luciano Pavarotti

29. B – Dean Martin

30. C – Tommy Dorsey

31. B – George Frideric Handel

32. D – Enrico Caruso

Did You Know: *As a youth in his native Naples he fell in love with a local girl. He wanted to marry her but the girl's father deemed him too low class and told him he would never amount to anything as an opera singer. A few years later he became the most famous singer in the world making himself a wealthy man.*

33. A – Cab Calloway

34. D – Hank Williams, Jr.

35. B – Mick Jagger

36. A – Garth Brooks

37. D – Paul McCartney

38. B – Tom Petty

39. B – Waylon Jennings

40. D – John Fogarty

41. B – Simon & Garfunkel

42. D – Wolfgang Amadeus Mozart

43. C – Ray Charles

44. A – Syd Barrett

45. C – Michael Jackson

46. B – Carlos Santana

47. A – Elvis Presley

48. D – Jimi Hendrix

49. C – Gene Krupa

50. A – Barry Gibb

51. B – Johann Sebastian Bach

Did You Know: *Bach had 20 children with his 2 wives. His first child arrived when he was 23 years of age and the last when Back was 57. Only 10 of his children would survive to adulthood. Many of them had musical abilities. His firstborn, Catharina, was an excellent singer. His oldest son, Wilhelm became a composer like his father. His fifth child, Carl Philipp, was the most gifted of his children. He was also a composer. He was also one of the foremost clavier players in Europe and was the leading keyboard teacher of his time. He was court musician to Frederick the Great and praised by none other than Mozart. His 6th child, Johann was a professional musician, but died in his early 20's. His 16th child & 9th son, (another son by the name of Johann but with a different middle name) Johann, played the harpsichord professionally and was a composer. And Johann's oldest son Wilhelm, was the only grandson of Bach to gain fame as a composer. His 18th child, Johann, (yes, his 3rd son with the name Johann. It seems he wasn't as creative in naming his children as he was in writing music)* *became a well-known classical composer and influenced Mozart's works.*

52. B – John Denver

53. C – Nat King Cole

54. A – Benny Goodman

55. C – Duke Ellington

56. B – Chuck Berry

57. C – Greg Allman

58. A – Ronnie Van Zant

59. B – Ludwig van Beethoven

60. C – Count Basie

21

Athletes

Answers for this chapter on page 203

1. On the official NBA website, it states that he is "the greatest basketball player of all time."

    A. Larry Bird   B. Shaquille O'Neal

    C. Michael Jordan   D. Magic Johnson

2. Which baseball player's rookie card sold for almost $100,000 – the highest price ever paid for a modern day baseball card? He was the first baseball player to be named All-Star MVP and World Series MVP in the same year.

    A. Barry Bonds   B. Derek Jeter

    C. Sandy Koufax   D. Alex Rodriguez

3. This professional boxer is widely regarded as one of the most significant and celebrated sports figures of the 20th century. He spouted such phases as "float like a butterfly, sting like a bee."

    A. George Foreman   B. Rocky Marciano

    C. Mohammed Ali   D. Joe Frazier

4. He has been called "the greatest hockey player ever" by sportswriters and the league. He has been dubbed "the great one."

    A. Wayne Gretzky   B. Bobby Orr

    C. Gordie Howe   D. Mario Lemieux

5. During his career in Major League baseball as a pitcher he had a record of 5,714 strikeouts and 7 no-hitters. He is considered one of the best pitchers of all time.

    A. Sandy Koufax   B. Nolan Ryan

    C. Cy Young   D. Randy Johnson

6. American swimmer who is the most decorated Olympian of all time. In 2008 he became the first athlete to win 8 gold medals at a single Olympics. He has set the record for winning the most medals, 28 total – 23 gold, 3 silver, and 2 bronze.

    A. Mark Spitz   B. Johnny Weismuller

    C. Luca Dotto   D. Michael Phelps

7. A former professional baseball and football player and the only athlete in history to be named All-Star in both football and baseball. He is widely considered one of the greatest athletes of all time.

    A. Deion Sanders   B. Bo Jackson

    C. Norm Bass   D. Cliff Aberson

8. This Swiss tennis player is one of the greatest tennis players in history having won a record of 20 Grand Slam singles titles – the most in history for a male player.

    A. Roger Federer   B. Bjorn Borg

C. John McEnroe   D. Andre Agassi

9. This professional baseball player had a career that spanned 22 seasons who fellow teammate Joe Dugan described as, "He wasn't human." He was baseball's first grand slugger and the most celebrated athlete of his time and to this day.

A. Hank Aaron   B. Babe Ruth

C. Ted Williams   D. Mickey Mantle

10. This Jamaican sprinter and world record holder is an Olympic legend and has been called "the fastest man alive." He is widely considered to be the greatest sprinter of all time.

A. Carl Lewis   B. Asafa Powell

C. Yohan Blake   D. Usain Bolt

11. A Brazilian footballer (or soccer player as they're called in America) who is regarded by many as "the greatest footballer of all time." In 1999, he was voted World Player of the Century.

A. Michel Platini   B. Ronaldo

C. Pelé   D. Garrincha

12. Which baseball player was a switch hitter, played in more games, had more at-bats, and more career hits than any other player in MLB history? He exceeded Ty Cobb's record for hits and was named Player of the Decade (1970 – '79), yet he's been banned from the Hall of Fame for life due to his gambling on sports teams (specifically he bet on the team he was managing at the time).

A. Mark McGwire   B. Pete Rose

C. Sammy Sosa   D. Shoeless Joe Jackson

13. This American track-and-field athlete won 4 gold medals at the 1936 Berlin Olympic games. He broke 2 world records, one which had held for 25 years. This Olympic athlete was the son of a sharecropper and the grandson of slaves. a furious Hitler stormed out of the Olympic games when his vision of Aryan supremacy was shattered at this athlete's dominating the field and breaking 2 world records. Who was he?

    A. Ralph Metcalfe   B. Cornelius "Corny" Johnson

    C. Jesse Owens   D. John Woodruff

14. A Spanish professional tennis player currently (as of 2018) ranked #1 in the world singles for men's singles.

    A. Rafael Nadal   B. Andre Agassi

    C. Roger Federer   D. José Acasuso

15. A baseball legend who is considered one of the greatest hitters of all time. His entire career he played with the Boston Red Sox.

    A. Jimmie Foxx   B. Carl Yastrzemski

    C. Roger Maris   D. Ted Williams

16. He is considered to be the greatest wide receiver in NFL history and often called the greatest NFL player of all time. He played primarily with the San Francisco 49ers, setting records for career touchdowns, receptions, and reception yardage.

    A. Lynn Swann   B. Jerry Rice

    C. Steve Largent   D. Don Hutson

17. American boxer who became the youngest heavyweight champion at the age of 20.

A. Evander Holyfield   B. Joe Frazier

C. Julio Cesar Chavez Jr.   D. Mike Tyson

18. This legend in baseball broke Babe Ruth's record of 714 home runs with his own record of 755 home runs. He is widely regarded as one of the baseball greats. His pro-career began just a few years after Jackie Robinson broke the color barrier.

A. Satchel Paige   B. Willie Mays

C. Hank Aaron   D. Bob Gibson

19. He was the first African American to play in Major League Baseball in the 20th century. He began playing with the Brooklyn Dodgers in 1947 and won Rookie of the Year the same year.

A. Barry Bonds   B. Jackie Robinson

C. Frank Thomas   D. Satchel Paige

20. American football quarterback who is considered to be one of the greatest quarterbacks of all time. He set numerous records, won 5 NFL MVP awards, and won 2 Super Bowls.

A. Peyton Manning   B. Fran Tarkenton

C. Brett Favre   D. Joe Montana

21. American professional boxer who is considered to be one of the greatest boxers of all time. He held the world welterweight title from 1946 – '51 and by 1958 became the first boxer to win a divisional world championship five times.

A. Sonny Liston   B. Jack Dempsey

C. Joe Louis   D. Sugar Ray Robinson

22. He is most remembered for his alleged association with the Black Sox Scandal in which members of the 1919 Chicago White Sox participated in a conspiracy to fix the World Series. Ultimately, he was then banned from the game.

    A. Shoeless Joe Jackson   B. Christy Mathewson

    C. Ray Fisher   D. Ty Cobb

23. He was the first NBA player to score more than 30,000 cumulative points over his career and the first and only player to date to have scored 100 points in a single game.

    A. Kobe Bryant   B. Wilt Chamberlain

    C. Larry Bird   D. Kareem Abdul-Jabbar

24. This Native American was dubbed "one of the greatest athletes of all time." He was excellent at every sport he ever tried, but gained his greatest fame by winning the decathelon and pentathlon events at the 1912 Olympics only to have his medals taken away (and later restored posthumously) for having once been paid to play minor league baseball.

    A. Jim Thorpe   B. Billy Mills

    C. Ellison "Tarzan" Brown   D. Notah Begay III

25. He is the only quarterback to take his team to 5 Super Bowl victories, one of only two players to win 5 Super Bowls, and the only player to win them all playing for the same team (New England Patriots).

    A. John Elway   B. Dan Marino

    C. Tom Brady   D. Otto Graham

26. He is the only world heavyweight champion in professional boxing history to retire undefeated.

A. Joe Louis　　　　　　　B. Evander Holyfield

　　C. Mike Tyson　　　　　　D. Rocky Marciano

27. This professional baseball player played with the New York Yankees for his entire career during the 1920's and '30's. He led the team to 6 World Series titles and set the mark for most consecutive games played. He retired after being diagnosed with ALS.

　　A. Bob Meusel　　　　　　B. Babe Ruth

　　C. Lou Gehrig　　　　　　 D. Joe DiMaggio

28. Nicknamed "The King," he was one of golf's most popular stars and regarded as not only one of the greats, but one of the most charismatic.

　　A. Jack Nicklaus　　　　　 B. Arnold Palmer

　　C. Ben Hogan　　　　　　 D. Bobby Jones

29. This baseball player's legacy as a pitcher is unlikely to ever be matched. He won 511 games during his career in baseball, almost 100 games more than any other pitcher. In 1904, he pitched the first perfect game of the 20th century.

　　A. Cy Young　　　　　　　B. Warren Spahn

　　C. Sandy Koufax　　　　　 D. Bob Feller

30. He was a Nascar driver who won a record-tying 7 Nascar championships before his death from crashing during the final lap of the Daytona 500 in 2001.

　　A. Cale Yarborough　　　　B. Donnie Allison

　　C. Lee Petty　　　　　　　 D. Dale Earnhardt

31. This professional golfer nicknamed "The Golden Bear," was a dominating figure in golf from the 1960's – '80's. He won 6 Masters Tournaments among his 18 career major championships, both professional records.

    A. Jack Nicklaus   B. Ben Hogan

    C. Sam Snead   D. Arnold Palmer

32. This professional baseball player played 21 seasons in Major League ball for the Baltimore Orioles. Nicknamed "The Iron Man," he established a record of 2,632 consecutive games played during his career.

    A. Ken Griffey, Jr.   B. Cal Ripken, Jr

    C. Reggie Jackson   D. Bo Jackson

33. A professional golfer who became the youngest man and the first African American to win the U.S. Masters.

    A. Robert Hawkins   B. John Shippen

    C. Tiger Woods   D. Harold Varner III

34. Which baseball player played all 21 years of his Major League career with the Kansas City Royals? His career hits of 3,154 are the most by any third baseman in Major League history. He is one of four players to accumulate 3,000 hits, 300 home runs, and a career 300 batting average. He's the only player in MLB history to win a batting title in 3 different decades.

    A. Bo Jackson   B. Tom Gordon

    C. George Brett   D. Greg Pryor

35. This Formula One race car driver is widely regarded as one of the greatest Formula One drivers of all time.

A. Michael Schumacher   B. Alain Prost

C. Fernando Alonso   D. Emerson Fittipaldi

36. He was a championship Nascar driver nicknamed "The King," who was the most successful driver in the history of the National Association for Stock Car Racing winning 200 races and 7 Winston cups.

A. Fireball Roberts   B. Bill Elliott

C. Cale Yarborough   D. Richard Petty

37. He is the professional baseball player who is regarded as the fiercest competitor in the game. He was one of the greatest offensive players in baseball history. He established numerous batting records, runs scored, and stolen bases. Many times his historic accomplishments weren't as celebrated as should have been due to his aggressiveness in playing and because of his temper, which don't take away from his accomplishments on the field.

A. Hank Aaron   B. Ty Cobb

C. Mickey Mantle   D. Ted Williams

38. This baseball player was nicknamed "The Flying Dutchman," and has been called the nearest thing to a perfect player (regardless of where his manager decided to play him). He played every position on the diamond in his major league career – except for catcher. He played 21 seasons, mostly with the Pittsburgh Pirates. He was one of the first 5 men elected to the Hall of Fame and considered by many as the best all-around player in the history of the National League. Many people today are familiar with him due to his baseball card being the rarest, most sought after, and worth millions.

A. Honus Wagner   B. Mickey Mantle

C. Roberto Clements   D. Shoeless Joe Jackson

39. This American boxer is the only professional fighter to win the heavyweight championship 4 times. In a fight in 1996 his ear was bitten by Mike Tyson.

    A. George Foreman   B. Muhammed Ali

    C. Evander Holyfield   D. Sugar Ray Leonard

40. A running back for the Cleveland Browns in the National Football League who is considered to be the greatest football player of all time.

    A. Jim Brown   B. Emmitt Smith

    C. George Pryor   D. Gale Sayers

41. He was one of the greatest baseball players in history with a 22-year major league career. He accomplished all 5 things you have to do well to become a superstar: hit, hit with power, run, throw, and field. He played 21 seasons with the Giants and ended his career with the Mets. He hit more than 600 home runs.

    A. Barry Bonds   B. Willie Mays

    C. Mickey Mantle   D. Ted Williams

42. This baseball star was nicknamed "Junior" and "The Kid." He was one of the most prolific home run hitters in baseball's history, ranking 7th most in MLB history. He won 10 Gold Glove Awards.

    A. Alex Rodriguez   B. Stan Musial

    C. Cal Ripken, Jr   D. Ken Griffey, Jr

43. This professional football player led the 49ers to victories in 4 Super Bowls. He is arguably the best quarterback in history and ranked #4 in a list of the game's all-time 100 players compiled by the NFL Network.

A. Tom Brady   B. John Elway

C. Joe Montana   D. Joe Namath

44. He was the baseball player known as "The Mick" who won 4 home run championships, a Triple Crown (highest batting average, most home runs, and most RBI's in 1 season), and 3 Most Valuable Player Awards during his 18 year career with the New York Yankees. He was considered the fastest man in baseball during the 1950's.

A. Mickey Mantle   B. Babe Ruth

C. Joe DiMaggio   D. Lou Gehrig

45. He was the pitcher who became the oldest rookie in Major League history – debuting at the age of 42.

A. Nolan Ryan   B. Satchel Paige

C. Julio Franco   D. Roger Clemens

46. He is widely considered to be the greatest wide receiver in NFL history and is often called the greatest NFL player of all time.

A. Lynn Swann   B. Steve Largent

C. Don Hutson   D. Jerry Rice

47. He is the Hall-of-Fame basketball player who holds the title of NBA's all-time leading scorer.

A. Michael Jordan   B. Kareem Abdul-Jabbar

C. LeBron James   D. Wilt Chamberlain

48. This professional athlete played both baseball and football professionally and is the only athlete to play in a Super Bowl and the World Series.

    A. Deion Sanders   *B. Bo Jackson*

    C. John Elway   *D. Tim Tebow*

49. What professional basketball player was the best Celtics player of all time?

    A. Kevin McHale   *B. Robert Parish*

    C. Bill Russell   *D. Larry Bird*

50. He was a professional football player who played with the Chicago Bears earning 9 Pro Bowl selections and set several rushing records. He is considered "one of the greats" in NFL history.

    A. Johnny Unitas   *B. Walter Payton*

    C. Tom Brady   *C. Peyton Manning*

Answers - Chapter 21 – Athletes

1. C – Michael Jordan

2. B – Derek Jeter

3. C – Mohammed Ali

4. A – Wayne Gretzky

5. B – Nolan Ryan

6. D – Michael Phelps

7. B – Bo Jackson

8. A – Roger Federer

9. B – Babe Ruth

10. D – Usain Bolt

11. C – Pelé

12. B – Pete Rose

13. C – Jesse Owens

14. A – Rafael Nadal

15. D – Ted Williams

16. B – Jerry Rice

17. D – Mike Tyson

18. C – Hank Aaron

Did You Know: *He lived to see the day when Barry Bonds broke his record and while not there for the event, a previously taped message from Aaron was put up on the scoreboard in which the message read, "I move over now and offer my best wishes to Barry and his family on this historic achievement." Barry's homerun record is discredited by many due to his having used performance enhanement drugs to achieve* that accomplishment; hence his achievements (Bonds) were tainted with steroids.

19. B – Jackie Robinson

20. A – Peyton Manning

21. D – Sugar Ray Robinson

22. A – Shoeless Joe Jackson

23. B – Wilt Chamberlain

24. A – Jim Thorpe

25. C – Tom Brady

26. D – Rocky Marciano

27. C – Lou Gehrig

28. B – Arnold Palmer

29. A – Cy Young

30. D – Dale Earnhardt

31. A – Jack Nicklaus

32. B – Cal Ripken, Jr

33. C – Tiger Woods

34. C – George Brett

35. A – Michael Schumacher

36. D – Richard Petty

37. B – Ty Cobb

38. A – Honus Wagner

39. C – Evander Holyfield

40. A – Jim Brown

41. B – Willie Mays

42. D – Ken Griffey, Jr

43. C – Joe Montana

44. A – Mickey Mantle

45. B – Satchel Paige

Did You Know: *With African American players barred from the Major Leagues, he began his career in the Negro League. In 1948 his dream came true with the color barrier broken by Jackie Robinson. When the Cleveland Indians were in need of a pitcher his own opportunity came. Paige was the 1st black pitcher in the American League and the 7th black to play Major League ball, and the 1st black pitcher to be inducted into Baseball's Hall Of Fame. Yankees Joe DiMaggio called him "the best and fastest pitcher I've ever faced."*

46. D – Jerry Rice

47. B – Kareem Abdul-Jabbar

48. A – Deion Sanders

49. D – Larry Bird

50. B – Walter Payton

22

Men Of War

Answers for this chapter on page 218

1. As Britain's prime minister he forged alliances with the U.S. and the Soviet Union to defeat Nazi Germany during WWII.

    A. Neville Chamberlain   B. Winston Churchill

    C. Robert Walpole   D. Benjamin Disraeli

2. He was an American war hero of WWI, a man who single-handedly captured 132 enemy soldiers.

    A. Daniel Daly   B. Frank Luke

    C. Charles Whittlesey   D. Alvin York

3. This man of war founded the Mongol Empire and conquered nearly 12 million square miles of territory (an area about the size of the entire continent of Africa), more than any other individual in history. He was one of the most feared conquerors of all times. He died at the age of 65 in the year 1227.

    A. Alexander the Great   B. Attila the Hun

    C. Genghis Khan   D. Timur (Tamerlane)

4. This outspoken and opioniated general was referred to as "Old Blood-and-Guts" by his men. America's greatest combat general of WWII, he began his military career leading cavalry troops against Mexican forces. He became the first officer assigned to the new tank corps during WWI. In WWII his forces played a key role in defeating the Germans at the Battle of the Bulge and then went on to capture 10,000 miles of territory liberating the country of the Nazi regime.

    A. Douglas MacArthur   B. Dwight D. Eisenhower

    C. Omar Bradley   D. George S. Patton

5. He served as the only President of the Confederate States from 1861 – 1865.

    A. Jefferson Davis   B. Stonewall Jackson

    C. George Meade   D. William Tecumseh Sherman

6. He was a Thracian gladiator (73 – 71 B.C.) who escaped and let a major slave uprising against the Roman Republic.

    A. Marcus Atilius   B. Commodus

    C. Spartacus   D. Russell Crowe

7. Twice he was rejected for war service, but he went on to become an American war hero and became the most decorated U.S. soldier of WWII earning 21 medals including the Congressional Medal of Honor.

    A. Eugene Fluckey   B. David McCampbell

    C. Desmond Doss   D. Audie Murphy

8. He was America's most successful and most well-known fighter ace in WWI. At the end of the war he had the most kills of any American pilot.

A. Theodore Roosevelt, Jr.   B. James Doolittle

C. Eddie Rickenbacker   D. Kenneth Walsh

9. He was the leader of the Nazi Party, chancellor, and Führer of Germany.

A. Hermann Goering   B. Adolf Hitler

C. Joseph Mengele   D. Heinrich Himmler

10. He crowned himself Emperor of France in 1804, and conquered much of Europe in the 19th century expanding his empire. His military strategy was led to a disastrous end when he and his army invaded Russia in 1812.

A. Benito Mussolini   B. Hideki Tojo

C. Peter the Great   D. Napoleon Bonaparte

11. He is considered the greatest general the world has ever known. He was undefeated in battle. He ruled the largest empire of the ancient world. He was considered one of history's greatest minds. He became "king of the four quarters of the known world," and accomplished this by the age of 32.

A. Cyrus the Great   B. Attila the Hun

C. Alaric the Visigoth   D. Alexander the Great

12. He was a wartime Japanese doctor who instead of healing he is responsible for tens of thousands of deaths. He was in charge of a massive biological warfare research program of the Japanese Imperial Army – he was the perpetrator of the Asian holocaust.

A. Hideki Tojo   B. Isoroku Yamamoto

C. Shirō Ishii   D. Heitaro Kimura

13. He was a British naval officer and the last viceroy of India, a member of the royal family (his great-grandmother was Queen Victoria, his father a prince, and his mother a Hessian princess). He served during WWI and WWII. In 1943, he became the Supreme Allied Commander and in 1945 received the Japanese surrender. He was murdered by the IRA.

    A. Neville Chamberlain   B. Lord Mountbatten

    C. Prince Philip   D. Prince George, Duke of Kent

14. He was a Revolutionary War hero, a general in the Continental Army, and was the founder and leader of the Green Mountain Boys.

    A. Ethan Allen   B. George Washington

    C. Henry Knox   D. Alexander Hamilton

15. He was a lifelong military man who during WWII served as Supreme Allied Commander and was commander of the D-Day invasion.

    A. Ferdinand Foch   B. Lynde McCormick

    C. John Pershing   D. Dwight D. Eisenhower

16. He served as Commander-in-Chief of the Continental Army during the American Revolutionary War.

    A. Charles Cornwallis   B. George Washington

    C. Henry Clinton   D. Nathanael Greene

17. He was the leading Confederate general during the American Civil War.

    A. Robert E. Lee   B. Ulysses S. Grant

    C. Jefferson Davis   D. Stonewall Jackson

18. He was commander of the U.S. Pacific Fleet during WWII. He commanded all land and sea forces in the central Pacific. His background was in submarines and his use of the "Silent Service" was extremely effective during WWII.

    A. Slade D. Cutter   B. Erich Topp

    C. Chester Nimitz   D. Charles Lockwood

19. He commanded the Union army during the Civil War and was one of the greatest generals in American history. Under his leadership the Union army was victorious.

    A. Robert E. Lee   B. Ulysses S. Grant

    C. George Meade   D. George Custer

20. In WWI this French general became a hero after his victory at the Battle of Verdun, but after returning from retirement in WWII he was charged with treason and jailed for the remainder of his life.

    A. Philippe Pétain   B. Charles de Gaulle

    C. Napoleon Bonaparte   D. Ferdinand Foch

21. He was a key figure behind the Holocaust. He was the second most powerful man in the Third Reich. He oversaw the construction of extermination camps and directed the killings of 6 million Jews and other ethnic groups deemed "undesirables" during the war. In other words, he was a genocidal killer.

    A. Adolf Eichmann   B. Heinrich Himmler

    C. Reinhard Heydrich   D. Erwin Rommel

22. He is one of Scotland's greatest national heroes, a patriot, and leader of the Scottish resistance forces during the struggle to free Scotland from

English rule.

 A. Edward I   B. Robert the Bruce

 C. Rob Roy MacGregor   D. William Wallace

23. He was a Roman general, politician, and consul seven times (157 B.C. - 86 B.C.) and was one of the Roman Republic's most accomplished men who was given credit for saving Rome from the brink of collapse.

 A. Pompey   B. Gaius Marius

 C. Marcus Crassus   D. Spartacus

24. He was Prime Minister of Prussia and as a leader of the Nazi Party he created the Gestapo as a Prussian police force. He later turned the Gestapo over to Himmler. In 1939, Hitler declared him as his successor and he was given the rank of Marshal of the Empire.

 A. Rudolf Hess   B. Bonaparte II

 C. Herman Goering   D. Joseph Goebbels

25. He invaded England in the year 1066 when the promise made to him by King Edward to make him heir went unfulfilled when Harold II ascended to the throne instead. He won the Battle of Hastings and became king. He made Britain one of the most powerful nations in Europe.

 A. Richard I   B. Edward the Confessor

 C. Robin Hood   D. William the Conqueror

26. He was the U.S. general who commanded the Southwest Pacific Theatre during WWII, he oversaw the Allied occupation of postwar Japan, and was in charge of UN forces during the Korean War.

A. Douglas MacArthur   B. Dwight D. Eisenhower

C. George Patton   D. Omar Bradley

27. He was a French general who led the French Resistance against the Nazis during WWII.

A. Marechal de Lattre de Tassigny   B. Charles de Gaulle

C. Jean Lafitte   D. Philippe Leclerc de Hauteclocque

28. He was a Muslim military and political leader who led the Islamic forces during the Crusades. He is a famous hero of the Muslims who captured Jerusalem.

A. Saladin   B. Yusuf Islam

C. Rumi   D. Shah Jahan

29. He was a Confederate general in the Civil War who earned his nickname at the First Battle of Bull Run.

A. Bloody Bill Anderson   B. Ambrose Burnside

C. Fighting Joe Hooker   D. Stonewall Jackson

30. He was the Nazi official responsible for overseeing the deportation of European Jews to extermination camps.

A. Heinrich Himmler   B. Adolf Eichmann

C. Hermann Göring   D. Joseph Goebbels

31. He was a Mexican revolutionary who fought for guerilla actions during and after the Mexican Revolution (1910 – '20).

A. Emiliano Zapata   B. Santa Anna

C. Benito Juárez   D. Carlos Santana

32. He was Japan's Marshal Admiral of the Navy and Commander-in-Chief of the Combined Fleet during WWII. He was responsible for the attack on Pearl Harbor and Midway.

A. Hirohito   B. Isoroku Yamamoto

C. Chūichi Nagumo   D. Hideki Tojo

33. He was called the "Angel of Death," though there was nothing angelic about this Nazi physician who was infamous for performing grisly human experiments on those imprisoned at the concentration camps.

A. Joseph Goebbels   B. Heinrich Himmler

C. Rudolf Hess   D. Joseph Mengele

34. He was called "Hero of the Two Worlds" due to his military campaigns in Latin America and Europe. In Italy he played a leading role in Italy's unification.

A. Giuseppe Garibaldi   B. Benito Mussolini

C. Cesare Mele   D. Rodolfo Graziani

35. He was commander of the First Army in WWII's Normandy campaign. This 5-star general became the first chairman of the Joint Chiefs of Staff.

A. John Pershing   B. Bernard Montgomery

C. Omar Bradley   D. Douglas MacArthur

36. He was Hitler's infamous minister of propaganda. Shortly before Hitler's suicide he appointed this man as the German chancellor.

    A. Rudolf Hess   B. Joseph Goebbels

    C. Claus Von Stauffenberg   D. Friedrich Fromm

37. Which son of a president was the only general involved, boots on the ground, in the initial assault on D-Day?

    A. David Eisenhower II   B. Alan Hoover

    C. Harry Garfield   D. Theodore Roosevelt, Jr

38. He is most remembered for defeating Robert E. Lee's Army at Gettysburg the bloodiest battle of the Civil War after having only been in command of the Union Army of the Potomac for 3 days.

    A. John Buford   B. Joshua Chamberlain

    C. George Meade   D. George Custer

39. He was a Revolutionary war hero known as the "Father of the U.S. Navy." He was one of the bravest soldiers in the Revolutionary Army. His famous words during the naval Battle of Flamborough Head when the British asked if he was ready to surrender he responded with, "I have not yet begun to fight!" He inspired others in their fight for independence and is still remembered as one of the most daring and successful naval commanders.

    A. David Farragut   B. John Paul Jones

    C. Oliver Hazard Perry   D. George Dewey

40. He was a British naval commander and national hero famous for his naval victories against the French during the Napoleonic Wars.

A. Horatio Nelson   B. Cuthbert Collingwood

C. Francis Drake   D. Leif Larsen

41. He was a general and dictator who ruled over Spain from 1939 until his death in 1975. He overthrew the Spanish democratic republic in the Spanish Civil War and ruled with a brutal dictatorship.

A. Benito Mussolini   B. Juan Carlos I

C. Augusto Pinochet   D. Francisco Franco

42. He was a soldier, politician, and a hero of the Irish in their struggle for independence. He was a member of Sinn Féin, he joined the Irish and Republican Brotherhood, and is most famous for his leadership of the republican military campaign against Britain in a War for Independence through the IRA (Irish Republican Army). He became one of the two most powerful men in Republican Ireland.

A. Michael Collins   B. Rory O'Connor

C. Liam Lynch   D. Martin McGuinness

43. He served in the Civil War and the Indian Wars. He is best known for his actions at the Battle of Little Bighorn in 1876 where 500 U.S. soldiers initiated the attack against 3,500 Indian warriors. All the U.S. troops were killed.

A. Zebulon Pike   B. George Crook

C. George Custer   D. Frank North

44. He was a German WWII Field Marshal of the North African campaign. He was known as the "Desert Fox."

A. George Patton   B. Adolf Hitler

C. Erwin Rommel   D. Napoleon Bonaparte

45. Manfred von Richthofen a German fighter pilot who few know of his given name, but instead know of him and his reputation by his nickname given him. He flew for the German Air Force during WWI and is considered the ace-of-aces of the war who is credited with 80 air combat victories.

A. Balloon Buster   B. Eagle of Crimea

C. Black Swallow of Death   D. Red Baron

46. From 10 Downing Street on Sept. 3, 1939 in a radio broadcast he announced to Britain that the country was at war with Germany.

A. Adolf Hitler   B. Winston Churchill

C. Neville Chamberlain   D. George VI

47. During WWII this fascist prime minister of Italy allied Italy with Nazi Germany.

A. Victor Emmanuel III   B. Benito Mussolini

C. Francisco Franco   D. Umberto II

48. He was a Carthaginian general during the Second Punic War between Carthage and Rome in the years 218 – 202 B.C. He proved himself to be one of the greatest military commanders in history. He is most remembered for using war elephants to intimidate his enemy on the battlefield.

A. Pyrrhus of Epirus   B. Constantine the Great

C. Hannibal   D. Spartacus

49. This dictator of the Soviet Socialist Republic (U.S.S.R.) aligned with the U.S. and Britain during WWII, but afterwards had a tense relationship with the West in what is known as the Cold War.

    A. Joseph Stalin　　　　　*B. Nikita Khrushchev*

    C. Vladimir Lenin　　　　　*D. Leonid Brezhnev*

50. He was a Roman general and was considered one of the greatest military minds in history. He turned the Roman Republic into the powerful Roman Empire.

    A. Alexander the Great　　　*B. Julius Caesar*

    C. Nero　　　　　　　　　*D. Pompey*

Answers - Chapter 22 – Men Of War

1. B – Winston Churchill

2. D – Alvin York

3. C – Genghis Khan

4. D – George Patton

5. A – Jefferson Davis

6. C – Spartacus

7. D – Audie Murphy

8. C – Eddie Rickenbacker

Did You Know: *Before the war he was one of the world's top race car drivers.*

9. B – Adolf Hitler

10. D – Napoleon Bonaparte

11. D – Alexander the Great

12. C – Shirō Ishii

13. B – Lord Mountbatten

14. A – Ethan Allen

15. D – Dwight D. Eisenhower

16. B – George Washington

17. A – Robert E. Lee

18. C – Chester Nimitz

19. B – Ulysses S. Grant

20. A – Philippe Pétain

21. B – Heinrich Himmler

22. D – William Wallace

23. B – Gaius Marius

24. C – Hermann Göring

25. D – William the Conqueror

26. A – Douglas MacArthur

27. B – Charles de Gaulle

28. A – Saladin

29. D – Stonewall Jackson

30. B – Adolf Eichmann

31. A – Emiliano Zapata

32. B – Isoroku Yakamoto

33. D – Joseph Mengele

34. A – Giuseppe Garibaldi

Did You Know: *He led successful military campaigns in Latin America and Europe. He became known as the "Hero of Two Worlds." His life was dedicated to Italy's unity, but he was interested in democracy worldwide. Italian patriot and soldier that through his conquest of Sicily and Naples with his guerilla Redshirts he greatly contributed to the achievement of Italian Unification in the mid-1800's. At the outbreak of the Civil War in America he was held in such high regard he was offered a command in the Union Army.*

35. C – Omar Bradley

36. B – Joseph Goebbels

37. D – Theodore Roosevelt, Jr.

Did You Know: *He was the son of President Theodore Roosevelt. He insisted to his superiors that he be one of the first men off the boats to lead and encourage the men on D-Day. Already crippled from fighting in WWI and with a heart condition at 56* *years of age and in his condition he was denied for taking any part of a battle that was considered a suicide mission. He was denied twice but at his insistence he won the battle. He thought the men seeing a general willing to go in would boost morale. On June 6, 1944, he led the Fourth Infantry Division's landing on Utah Beach. With a limp and a bad heart, both he and his son Quentin Roosevelt II, the only father-son duo to fight on D-Day led with honor. Armed with only a cane and a pistol he led the men up the beach and stood there with bullets whizzing by his head encouraging the men. He miraculously survived the battle but died a month later from a heart attack.*

38. C – George Meade

39. B – John Paul Jones

40. A – Horatio Nelson

41. D – Francisco Franco

42. A – Michael Collins

43. C – George Custer

44. C – Erwin Rommel

45. D – Red Baron

46. C – Neville Chamberlain

47. B – Benito Mussolini

48. C – Hannibal

49. A – Joseph Stalin

50. B – Julius Caesar

23

Political Leaders & Heads of State

Answers for this chapter on page 230

1. He is the current president of Russia (as of 2018).

    A. Mikhail Gorbachev   B. Boris Yeltsin

    C. Vladimir Putin   D. Nikita Khrushchev

2. He is the current president of France (as of 2018).

    A. Emmanuel Macron   B. Jacques Chirac

    C. François Mitterrand   D. François Hollande

3. He was the ruthless dictator and president of Iraq from 1979 – 2003.

    A. Muammar Gaddafi   B. Osama bin Laden

    C. Bashar al-Assad   D. Saddam Hussein

4. Regarded as one of the greatest revolutionary leaders in history, he

was the founder of the Russian Communist Party, leader of the Bolshevik Revolution, and the first head of the Soviet State. He was master-mind of the Bolshevik takeover of power and to secure that position it is strongly believed that it was he who had the tzar and his family murdered by a Bolshevik firing squad.

A. Joseph Stalin

B. Vladimir Lenin

C. Vyacheslav Molotov

D. Yuri Andropov

5. He was the first prime minister of India and a leader of the Indian independence movement.

A. Bhagat Singh

B. Subhas Chandra Bose

C. Lal Bahadur Shastri

D. Jawaharlal Nehru

6. He orchestrated the Cuban Revolution taking over Cuba by force in 1959. He remained in control for nearly half a century. He transformed Cuba into the first communist state in the Western Hemisphere.

A. Fulgencio Batista

B. Hugo Chávez

C. Fidel Castro

D. Che Guevara

7. As dictator of the U.S.S.R. he ruled the Soviet Union for over two decades instituting a reign of terror, while at the same time modernizing Russia. His forced industrialization of the Soviet Union caused the worst manmade famine in history. He aligned with the U.S. and the United Kingdom during WWII.

A. Joseph Stalin

B. Leon Trotsky

C. Karl Marx

D. Konstantin Chernenko

8. In 1979 he led the revolution that overthrew the Shah of Iran and made Iran the world's first Islamic republic in which he became Iran's political

and religious leader.

    A. Reza Shah   B. Ruhollah Khomeini

    C. Mahmoud Ahmadinejad   D. Mohammad Reza Pahlavi

9. He led a rebellion during the Spanish Civil War in 1936 – '39 establishing himself as dictator exerting absolute control over the country.

    A. Francisco Franco   B. Luis Carrero Blanco

    C. Alfonso XIII   D. Juan Carlos I

10. He became the de facto leader of Libya following a bloodless coup d'état.

    A. Hosni Mubarak   B. Idi Amin

    C. Muammar Gaddafi   D. Gamal Abdel Nasser

11. He was the leader of the Chinese Nationalist Party and known as "The Father of Modern China."

    A. Kai-Shek Chiang   B. Mao Zedong

    C. Li Yuanhong   D. Sun Yat-sen

12. He was an English soldier who led the parliamentary forces in the English Civil War. He became the most successful military and political leader of the Civil War. He became Lord Protector of England, Wales, Scotland, and Ireland from 1653 – 1658. He was offered the crown and refused it, being a king in all but name and was addressed as "Your Highness."

    A. Oliver Cromwell   B. John Locke

C. Thomas Fairfax   D. Charles I

13. He transformed a collection of small German states into the German Empire and under his leadership ruled Prussia and then all of Germany. He was the founder and first chancellor of the German Empire from 1871 – 1890.

   A. William I   B. Paul von Hindenburg

   C. Otto von Bismarck   D. Kaiser Wilhelm II

14. He was the first freely elected leader in Russia's 1,000-year history. President for nearly 9 years he surprised the world when he announced his resignation, but in addition to health problems he said he decided Russia needed a new leader to usher in the new millenium.

   A. Yuri Andropov   B. Nikita Khrushchev

   C. Mikhail Gorbachev   D. Boris Yeltsin

15. He served as president of the Republic of China between 1928 – 1975, recognized by most of the world as the legitimate head of the government of China even though he was in exile.

   A. Sun Yat-sen   B. Puyi

   C. Chiang Kai-shek   D. Mao Zedong

16. He was founder of the Indochina Communist Party, the Viet Minh, and president of North Vietnam from 1945 – 1969.

   A. Võ Nguyên Giáp   B. Ho Chi Minh

   C. Nguyễn Văn Thiệu   D. Bảo Đại

17. He is the current prime minister of Canada (as of 2018).

    A. Justin Trudeau   B. Jean Chrétien

    C. Stephen Harper   D. Pierre Trudeau

18. He is the current president of China (as of 2018) and the only Chinese president to have a PhD. One reform he has made since becoming president is to change the one-child policy, allowing two children per family.

    A. Li Xiannian   B. Kim Jong-un

    C. Xi Jinping   D. Hu Jintao

19. He was a Palestinian leader and chairman of the PLO. He along with Peres of Israel was awarded the Nobel Prize for Peace in 1994 for leading the PLO to a peace agreement with the Israeli government.

    A. Anwar Sadat   B. Yasser Arafat

    C. Ariel Sharon   D. Benjamin Netanyahu

20. Four times he served as Prime Minister of the United Kingdom during the late 1800's. He is one of the longest serving and one of the most controversail British politicians. He started as a Tory and ended his career as a Liberal. He was a passionate campaigner for home rule for Ireland in the Victorian era.

    A. William Gladstone   B. Arthur Wellesley

    C. David Lloyd George   D. Benjamin Disraeli

21. He spent the longest time in office of any French president, 1981 – 1995 and was the first figure from the left to serve as president under the Fifth Republic.

A. Charles de Gaulle   B. François Hollande

C. François Mitterrand   D. Jacques Chirac

22. He was the last Emperor of Russia, ruling from 1894 until he was forced to abdicate in 1917.

A. Peter the Great   B. Nicholas II

C. Alexander I   D. Grigori Rasputin

23. Other than the French king himself, he was one of the most well-known and most influential figures associated with the French Revolution and the Reign of Terror.

A. Jean-Jacques Rousseau   B. Jean-Paul Marat

C. Georges Danton   D. Maximilien de Robespierre

24. He was a Venezuelan military leader instrumental in the revolution against the Spanish Empire, helping Latin American countries achieve independence.

A. Francisco de Miranda   B. Simón Bolívar

C. Giuseppe Garibaldi   D. José Antonio Páez

25. He served twice as prime minister of the United Kingdom and is known for securing the transformation of his country into an imperial power.

A. Spencer Perceval   B. Henry Pelham

C. William Pitt the Elder   D. Robert Walpole

26. He was president of Venezuela from 1999 – 2013. He was one of the most controversial figures in Latin America who was responsible for today's crisis in Venezuela created by his revolutionary plan.

    A. Hugo Chávez   B. Che Guevara

    C. Cesar Chavez   D. Nicolás Maduro

27. He is the current president of Syria (as of 2018).

    A. Hosni Mubarak   B. Bashar al-Assad

    C. Abdul Halim Khaddam   D. Saddam Hussein

28. He was President of Uganda from 1971 – '79 who was known as the "Butcher of Uganda," killing anywhere from 100,000 to half a million opponents.

    A. Mobutu Sese Seko   B. Nelson Mandela

    C. Idi Amin   D. Milton Obote

29. "Officially" he was the first Prime Minister of the United Kingdom and the youngest to have ever held the title. He was prime minister during the French Revolutionary and Napoleonic Wars.

    A. William Cavendish-Bentinck   B. Spencer Perceval

    C. William Wilberforce   D. William Pitt the Younger

30. He was President of Nicaragua from 1984 – 1990 and re-elected for 3 consecutive terms from 2007 – 2016. Before becoming president he was a guerilla leader and Sandinista. He was elected president despite President Reagan's and the CIA's attempt to overthrow him and the Sandanista Party.

    A. Daniel Ortega   B. Augusto Pinochet

C. Hugo Chávez   D. Manuel Noriega

31. He is the current Prime Minister of Hungary (as of 2018) and has held that position since 2010.

    A. Gordon Bajnai   B. Miloš Zeman

    C. Viktor Orbán   D. George Soros

32. Three times he was elected as President of Argentina, 1946 – 1955 and 1973 – 1974.

    A. Carlos Lacoste   B. Juan Perón

    C. Néstor Kirchner   D. Jorge Rafael Videla

33. He started off as a bus driver, became a trade union leader, and is the current President of Venezuela (as of 2018).

    A. Carlos Andrés Pérez   B. Leopoldo López

    C. Nicolás Maduro   D. Christopher Columbus

34. He is the current Emperor of Japan (as of 2018).

    A. Akihito   B. Hirohito

    C. Shinzō Abe   D. Jimmu

35. He was a Chinese communist revolutionary leader who became the founding father of the People's Republic of China.

    A. Chiang Kai-shek   B. Xi Jinping

    C. Ho Chi Minh   D. Mao Zedong

36. He was the primary national founder of the State of Israel and Israel's first prime minister.

    A. Ariel Sharon   B. David Ben-Gurion

    C. Benjamin Netanyahu   D. Jared Kushner

37. He is the current president of Iran (as of 2018) and has been serving as president since 2013.

    A. Hassan Rouhani   B. Ruhollah Khomeini

    C. Mahmoud Ahmadinejad   D. Ali Khamenei

38. He was Chancellor of West Germany from 1982 – '98 and the architect of the German reunification.

    A. Helmut Kohl   B. Horst Köhler

    C. Erich Honecker   D. Otto von Bismarck

39. He was President of Egypt from 1970 until his assassination in 1981. He is best remembered for initiating peace negotiations with Israel.

    A. Gamal Abdel Nasser   B. Farouk I

    C. Anwar Sadat   D. Hosni Mubarak

40. He was the Prime Minister of the United Kingdom who during WWII forged alliances with the U.S. and the Soviet Union in order to defeat Nazi Germany and led his country from the brink of defeat to victory.

    A. Neville Chamberlain   B. Winston Churchill

    C. Clement Attlee   D. Walter Raleigh

Answers - Chapter 23 – Political Leaders & Heads of State

1. C – Vladimir Putin

2. A – Emmanuel Macron

3. D – Saddam Hussein

4. B – Vladimir Lenin

5. D – Jawaharlal Nehru

6. C – Fidel Castro

7. A – Joseph Stalin

8. B – Ruhollah Khomeini

9. A – Francisco Franco

10. C – Muammar Gaddafi

11. D – Sun Yat-sen

12. A – Oliver Cromwell

Did You Know: *He died of malaria in 1658 and his oldest son succeeded him. Within a year of his death the Stuarts were restored to the monarchy. Parliament exhumed Cromwell's body for a posthumous execution of his corpse. His body was publicly hanged and beheaded with his head displayed on a spike above Westminster Hall remaining there for decades. In 1685 the spike broke and the head fell to the ground and remained there until it was discovered by a soldier who hid it in his chimney. On the soldier's deathbed he revealed to his daughter the story and whereabouts of Cromwell's skull. Years later (in 1710) the head was displayed in a freak show and in 1960 after exchanging hands many times for a fair amount of money the head found it's way to Cromwell's alma mater Sydney Sussex College and was buried on the college grounds in a secret location.*

13. C – Otto von Bismarck

14. D – Boris Yeltsin

15. C – Chiang Kai-shek

16. B – Ho Chi Minh

17. A – Justin Trudeau

18. C – Xi Jinping

19. B – Yasser Arafat

20. A – William Gladstone

21. C – François Mitterrand

22. B – Nicholas II

Did You Know: *It was during his reign that the fall of the Russian Empire occurred, seeing one of the foremost great powers of the world collapse. Tsar Nicholas II, Alexandra the Empress of Russia, their 5 children: Olga, Tatiana, Marie and Anastasia and a son Alexi who would have been the heir, and 4 servants were held prisoner and then executed by being shot, bayoneted, and clubbed to death and then disposed of in unmarked graves in the marshy forest near Yekaterinburg.*

23. D – Maximilien de Robespierre

24. B – Simón Bolívar

25. C – William Pitt the Elder

26. A – Hugo Chávez

27. B – Bashar al-Assad

28. C – Idi Amin

29. D – William Pitt the Younger

30. A – Daniel Ortega

31. C – Viktor Orbán

32. B – Juan Perón

33. C – Nicolás Maduro

34. A – Akhito

35. D – Mao Zedong (commonly known as Chairman Mao)

36. B – David Ben-Gurion

37. A – Hassan Rouhani

38. A – Helmut Kohl

39. C – Anwar Sadat

40. B – Winston Churchill

24

Presidents of the United States

Answers for this chapter on page 240

1. He was the first vice-president to become president after the death of his predecessor.

    A. Gerald Ford   B. Zachary Taylor

    C. John Tyler   D. Andrew Johnson

2. He is the only president in our nation's history who was a bachelor throughout his entire term as president. He was the president when the Pony Express began in 1860.

    A. James Buchanan   B. Grover Cleveland

    C. John Quincy Adams   D. Franklin Pierce

3. He was our only president who had also been Director of the CIA. He was president during Desert Storm and during the collapse of communism in the Soviet Union.

    A. George W. Bush   B. John F. Kennedy

C. Herbert Hoover   D. George H.W. Bush

4. He was president when Apollo 11 landed on the moon in 1969. He is also our only president who resigned before he could be impeached due to the scandal of Watergate.

    A. Bill Clinton   B. Richard Nixon

    C. Andrew Johnson   D. Donald Trump

5. He was president during the Civil War, he issued the Emancipation Proclamation, and was the first president to be assassinated.

    A. Abraham Lincoln   B. Ulysses S. Grant

    C. James Buchanan   D. James Garfield

6. The terrorist bombing at the Boston Marathon occured during his presidency. He was our nation's first African American president, though by the end of his presidency there was more racial division in our nation since the 1992 riots in Los Angeles during the Rodney King case and since back in the '60's when black Americans fought for equal rights. He had promised "Change" which gave great hope and high expectations for African Americans, though he was hugely disappointing in following though on his promises and instead it became one of his biggest failures.

    A. Warren Harding   B. Andrew Jackson

    C. Barack Obama   D. Andrew Johnson

7. He was the only president to have earned a doctrate. He was president when WWI broke out and when the 19th Amendment to the Constitution was implemented, allowing women the right to vote.

    A. William McKinley   B. Rutherford B. Hayes

    C. Harry Truman   D. Woodrow Wilson

8. Which president introduced the Bill of Rights and the first Ten Amendments to the Constitution? He was president during the War of 1812.

    A. James Monroe   B. James Madison

    C. Thomas Jefferson   D. John Adams

9. While he was president there was no vice-president, per his request.

    A. Chester Arthur   B. Calvin Coolidge

    C. Andrew Johnson   D. Benjamin Harrison

10. He began his presidency with the reputation of a "stolen election" due to the voting debacle. The beginning of America's worst financial crisis since the Great Depression began during his presidency. He was president during the 9/11 terrorist attacks killing about 3,000 people and he justified the War of Iraq by claiming they had weapons of mass destruction. He is ranked by historians as one of the top ten worst presidents in history.

    A. Bill Clinton   B. Jimmy Carter

    C. George H.W. Bush   D. George W. Bush

11. The stock market crash of 1929 happened during whose presidency, which brought about the Great Depression?

    A. Franklin D. Roosevelt   B. Millard Fillmore

    C. Herbert Hoover   D. Warren Harding

12. Which president was our only president to have been physically handicapped and served more than two terms? He was president when WWII broke out, when Pearl Harbor was attacked, he signed an executive order which authorized the military to relocate Japanese

Americans to internment camps, and had a waartime meeting with Churchill and Stalin to demand Germany's unconditional surrender.

    A. Harry Truman   B. Franklin D. Roosevelt

    C. Herbert Hoover   D. Theodore Roosevelt

13. Who was president when the first atomic bombs were dropped on Hiroshima and Nagasaki in the year 1945?

    A. Harry Truman   B. Franklin D. Roosevelt

    C. Dwight D. Eisenhower   D. John F. Kennedy

14. Who was president at the start of the California Gold Rush? He was the president who expanded the American territories to the Pacific Ocean, known as the Manifest Destiny.

    A. Martin Van Buren   B. Thomas Jefferson

    C. James Polk   D. Andrew Jackson

15. Who was president when Wilbur and Orville Wright first flew in 1903?

    A. Benjamin Harrison   B. Grover Cleveland

    C. William McKinley   D. Theodore Roosevelt

16. He was president when the "Golden Spike" was driven in 1869 joining the rails of the Transcontinental Railroad and when Custer's Last Stand took place.

    A. Rutherford B. Hayes   B. Chester Arthur

    C. Ulysses S. Grant   D. Franklin Pierce

17. Who was president when the U.S. purchased Alaska?

    A. Millard Fillmore   B. Andrew Johnson

    C. Grover Cleveland   D. Rutherford B. Hayes

18. He was president at the time of the Louisiana Purchase.

    A. Thomas Jefferson   B. James Madison

    C. James Monroe   D. Martin Van Buren

19. Who was president when the Trail of Tears, a forced relocation of Native Americans occurred?

    A. Andrew Johnson   B. Andrew Jackson

    C. Zachary Taylor   D. Martin Van Buren

20. Who was president when Charles Lindbergh flew the first solo transatlantic flight in 1927?

    A. William Howard Taft   B. Calvin Coolidge

    C. William McKinley   D. Woodrow Wilson

21. Who became the first unelected president, who had also been an unelected vice president?

    A. Richard Nixon   B. George W. Bush

    C. Lyndon B. Johnson   D. Gerald Ford

22. Which president was the only man to serve not only as president but also as chief justice?

A. Thomas Jefferson   B. James Madison

C. William Howard Taft   D. James Garfield

23. Which president joined with Mexico to strengthen border security?

A. Rutherford B. Hayes   B. Donald Trump

C. Ronald Reagan   D. Zachary Taylor

24. Which president signed peace treaties with Germany and Austria after WWI?

A. William Howard Taft   B. Woodrow Wilson

C. Warren Harding   D. Calvin Coolidge

25. He was our first president, Commander-in-Chief of the Continental Army during the Revolutionary War, and is known as the "Father of Our Country."

A. Thomas Jefferson   B. George Washington

C. James Madison   D. James Monroe

26. He served for the shortest time of any president. He died just 32 days after being sworn into office.

A. John Adams   B. John Tyler

C. John Quincy Adams   D. William Henry Harrison

27. He was the first businessman with no prior experience as a politician to be elected as president. That business sense was an asset to improving the economy and bringing more jobs to the American people. Many

people saw the American system as "broken" and in need of a fix and liked the fact that he wasn't a politician.

    A. John F. Kennedy   B. Ronald Reagan

    C. Donald Trump   D. Dwight D. Eisenhower

28. Who was president when America was presented the Statue of Liberty as a gift from France to commemorate the 100-year anniversary of the birth of liberty in the US. ?

    A. Grover Cleveland   B. William McKinley

    C. Theodore Roosevelt   D. Benjamin Harrison

29. Which president had been Supreme Allied Commander of WWII?

    A. Woodrow Wilson   B. Dwight D. Eisenhower

    C. John F. Kennedy   D. Theodore Roosevelt

30. He was an actor before becoming president, he introduced the Strategic Defense Initiative, he played a key role in ending the Cold War, his economic program led to one of the largest peacetime economic booms in U.S. history, and he is considered one of the most influential presidents in U.S. history.

    A. Abraham Lincoln   B. Franklin D. Roosevelt

    C. Bill Clinton   D. Ronald Reagan

Answers - Chapter 24 – Presidents of the United States

1. C – John Tyler

2. A – James Buchanan

Did You Know: *Grover Cleveland was a bachelor when he was elected, but was married during his first administration.*

3. D – George H.W. Bush

4. B – Richard Nixon

5. A – Abraham Lincoln

6. C – Barack Obama

7. D – Woodrow Wilson

8. B – James Madison

9. A – Chester Arthur

Did You Know: *Chester Arthur assumed the office of the presidency after the death of President James Garfield. Arthur requested a Senate special session to ensure that the Senate had legal authority to convene immediately and choose a Senate president pro tempore who would be able to assume the presidency if Arthur died during his administration.*

10. D – George W. Bush

11. C – Herbert Hoover

12. B – Franklin D. Roosevelt

13. A – Harry Truman

14. C – James Polk

15. D – Theodore Roosevelt

16. C – Ulysses S. Grant

17. B – Andrew Johnson

18. A – Thomas Jefferson

Did You Know: *The Louisiana Purchase was one of the most important land acquisitions ever made by the U.S., doubling the size of the U.S. Originally it was the purchase of New Orleans the U.S. sought after, due to the Mississippi River being the nation's primary port the U.S. feared France may one day close the port to America. When approached in reference to the sale of New Orleans, Napoleon needing funds to use the money to support his ongoing wars he agreed to not only selling New Orleans but quite a bit more. At pennies per acre it was the greatest land bargain in the history of America.*

19. D – Martin Van Buren

20. B – Calvin Coolidge

21. D – Gerald Ford

Did You Know: *He became vice-president and president while not elected to either office replacing Agnew as vice-president when he resigned and Nixon when he resigned – both resignations were due to scandal.*

22. C – William Howard Taft

Did You Know: *He was the only man in history to hold the highest position in not only the executive branch, but also the judicial branch of government.*

23. A – Rutherford B. Hayes

24. C – Warren Harding

25. B – George Washington

26. D – William Henry Harrison

27. C – Donald Trump

28. A – Grover Cleveland

29. B – Dwight D. Eisenhower

30. D – Ronald Reagan

25

Most Brutal Dictators In History

Answers for this chapter on page 246

1. The Prince of Wallachia, a region of Romania, who ruled from 1448 – 1476 earned the nickname "The Impaler" for impaling people on stakes and letting them die a long, painful death. It is estimated he is responsible for 40,000 – 100,000 deaths of his own people. Today he is more revered as a national hero as he came from the House of Drăculeşti and was the person associated with the story of Dracula.

    A. Bram Stoker   B. Vlad III

    C. Matthias Corvinus   D. Vladislav II of Wallachia

2. This dictator of the Russian Soviet Federative Socialist Republic and of the Soviet Union, he came to power by force after the end of the Romanov dynasty. He was the leader of the world's first communist state. He instituted a period known as the Red Terror, the executions of 590 people accused of involvement in the counterrevolutionary coup against the Hungarian Soviet Republic, and those who were supporters of the czarist regime.

    A. Leon Trotsky   B. Alexei Rykov

    C. Konstantin Chernenko   D. Vladimir Lenin

3. He was President of North Vietnam and America's #1 enemy during the Vietnam War. He was a brutal murderer dedicated to spreading communism throughout Asia, regardless of the cost. He and his henchmen are responsible for the deaths of over 26 million people.

    A. Ho Chi Minh   *B. Ngo Dinh Diem*

    C. Võ Nguyên Giáp   *D. Lê Duẩn*

4. The first Supreme Leader of North Korea, it was he who authorized the invasion of South Korea igniting the Korean War. He is considered "Eternal President of the Republic." He turned his country into an Orwellian state and is said to be responsible for as many as over 1,500,000 deaths.

    A. Kim Yong-nam   *B. Kim Jong-un*

    C. Kim Il-sung   *D. Kim Jong-il*

5. He was Communist leader of the Republic of China, the "Father of Chinese Communism." He reigned from 1949 – 1976. He was one of the worst mass murderers of the 20th century. An estimated 65 million Chinese died during his endeavours to create a socialist China.

    A. Mao Zedong, or Chairman Mao *B. Lin Biao*

    C. Zhao Ziyang   *D. Liu Shaoqi*

6. Following examples of his predecessors, this Soviet leader was responsible for the genocide against the Moldovians, Volga Germans, Polish, and Armenians.

    A. Yuri Andropov   *B. Leonid Brezhnev*

    C. Alexei Rykov   *D. Joseph Stalin*

7. A former Supreme Leader of North Korea and father to the current

leader, he was responsible for the starvation and deaths of millions of North Koreans.

  A. Kim Jong-il   B. Kim Tu-bong

  C. Kim Yong-nam   D. Kim Il-sung

8. This Iraqi dictator came to power in 1979 and remained in power until 2003 with the invasion of the U.S. and the United Kingdom. While in power he instituted mass genocide against certain ethnic groups such as the Kurds who rebelled against his leadership leaving an estimated 2 million dead.

  A. Augusto Pinochet   B. Bashar al-Assad

  C. Osama bin Laden   D. Saddam Hussein

9. This Spanish dictator led a military rebellion overthrowing Spain's democratic republic in the Spanish Civil War. Tens of thousands with some estimating it to be more in the hundreds of thousands were executed or imprisoned during his regime.

  A. Benito Mussolini   B. Francisco Franco

  C. Anastasio Somoza García D. Augusto Pinochet

10. He was a Haitian dictator who reigned from 1957 – 1971 using a cult he claimed had magical powers and voodoo torturing and killing thousands. He was known as "Papa Doc" and he was succeeded by his son after his death who continued his father's reign of terror.

  A. Rafael Trujillo   B. Jean-Jacques Dessalines

  C. François Duvalier   D. Daniel Fignolé

11. This leader of the Khmer Rouge and dictator of Cambodia from 1975 – 1979 was responsible for one of the severest genocides in modern history.

A. Pol Pot   B. Ta Mok

C. Nuon Chea   D. Kang Kek Iew

12. He was ruler of Uganda from 1971 – 1979 and it is estimated that he was responsible for anywhere from 300,000 – 500,000 deaths, earning him the nickname "The Butcher of Uganda."

A. Hissène Habré   B. Omar al-Bashir

C. Idi Amin   D. Sani Abacha

13. He rose to power after Lenin's death. He was known as a merciless dictator killing civilians and his own people – surpassing even Hitler in his murerous rule. He left a legacy of death and terror as he turned a backward Russia into a world superpower. During his reign "the Purge" took place, killing anyone who posed a threat to him.

A. Ivan IV the Terrible   B. Nicholas II

C. Sviatopolk the Accursed   D. Joseph Stalin

14. He was one of the most powerful and notorious dictators of the 20th century and leader of Germany's Nazi Party during WWII.

A. Hermann Göring   B. Adolf Hitler

C. Heinrich Himmler D. Joseph Goebbels

Answers - Chapter 25 – Most Brutal Dictators In History

1. B – Vlad III

2. D – Vladimir Lenin

3. A – Ho Chi Minh

4. C - Kim Il-sung

5. A – Mao Zedong, also known as Chairman Mao

Did You Know: *Some rural Chinese villages lost half of their citizens due to hunger during his rule. In just two years time the number of dead reached between 30 – 40 million; equivalent to the entire population of the state of California.*

6. B - Leonid Brezhnev

7. A - Kim Jong-il

8. D – Saddam Hussein

9. B – Francisco Franco

10. C - François Duvalier

11. A - Pol Pot

12. C – Idi Amin

13. D – Joseph Stalin

14. B – Adolf Hitler

26

Achievements Throughout History

Answers for this chapter on page 253

1. In 1785, this American physician joined French aviation pioneer Jean-Pierre Blanchard to become the first man to cross the English Channel by air in a hydrogen gas balloon.

  A. John Jeffries   B. Louis Blériot

  C. Benjamin Franklin   D. André-Jacques Garnerin

2. In 1786, the first private test of this man's new invention the steamboat takes place in the Delaware River.

  A. George Stephenson   B. DeWitt Clinton

  C. John Fitch   D. Elias Howe

3. In 1790 the first patent in the U.S. was issued to him for his improved method of potash.

  A. Samuel Clemens   B. Joseph Sampson

  C. Oliver Evans   D. Samuel Hopkins

4. On April 30, 1789 in New York City at Federal Hall he was sworn in as our nation's first president.

    A. Alexander Hamilton   B. Thomas Jefferson

    C. George Washington   D. James Madison

5. In 1794 he patented the cotton gin which did the work of 50 men.

    A. Samuel Morse   B. Eli Whitney

    C. James Watt   D. Cyrus McCormick

6. In 1804 these two men began their journey /expedition to map the Northwest United States exploring the newly acquired lands of the Louisiana Purchase, a two year four month long discovery expedition.

    A. Lewis & Clark   B. Boone & Crocket

    C. Johnson & Stroud   D. Carson & Adams

7. In 1806 this man published 'Webster's Dictionary,' the book which is credited for standardizing spelling and pronunciation.

    A. Daniel Webster   B. Arthur Gordon Webster

    C. John White Webster   D. Noah Webster

8. In 1807 the first practical steamboat journey was made by what man in the steamboat 'Clermont'? This became the first commercial steamboat service in the world.

    A. Edmund Cartwright   B. DeWitt Clinton

    C. Robert Fulton   D. John Marshall

9. In 1832 these two men led the first wagons across the Continental Divide at Wyoming's South Pass navigating 21 wagons and 110 men.

    A. Masters & Shannon   B. Bonneville & Walker

    C. Adams & Adams   D. Donner & Reed

10. In 1835 he began his first circus tour of the United States.

    A. James Bailey   B. John Ringling

    C. P.T. Barnum   D. Robert Ripley

11. In 1838 he first publicly demonstrated the telegraph and developed a code used for communication which was named for him.

    A. Samuel Morse   B. Thomas Edison

    C. Alexander Graham Bell   D. Louis Braille

12. In 1848 he discovered gold at Sutter's Mill.

    A. John Sutter   B. James Marshall

    C. John C. Frémont   D. George Hurst

13. In 1858 these two landscape architects won the competition and adoption of their plan for Central Park in New York City.

    A. Olmsted & Vaux   B. Olmstead & Downing

    C. Halprin & Wurster   D. Jencks & Banham

14. In 1897 the first Boston Marathon was run with 15 runners. This man was the winner of the first Boston Marathon.

A. Grete Waitz   B. Phidippides

C. Spiridon Louis   D. John McDermott

15. In 1909 this American explorer claimed to be the first person to reach the North Pole.

    A. Frederick Cook   B. Roald Amundsen

    C. Robert Peary   D. Richard E. Byrd

16. In 1911 he landed his plane on the deck of the *U.S.S. Pennsylvania* in the San Francisco Harbor for the first landing of a plane on a ship.

    A. Charles Lindbergh   B. Eugene Ely

    C. Charles Rumney Samson D. Robert Lee Scott Jr.

17. In 1911 the very first Indianapolis 500 auto race is run with this man as the winner.

    A. Ray Harroun   B. Jules Goux

    C. Louis Meyer   D. A. J. Foyt

18. In 1927 he made the first non-stop transatlantic flight in history.

    A. Henri Farman   B. Orville Wright

    C. Glenn Curtiss   D. Charles Lindbergh

19. In 1927 this sculptor began chiseling the busts of four presidents at Mount Rushmore.

    A. Daniel Chester   B. Frédéric Auguste Bartholdi

C. Gutzon Borglum   D. Paul Landowski

20. In 1947 who was the test pilot who became the first person to break the sound barrier.

   A. Chuck Yeager   B. John Glenn

   C. Sam Shepard   D. Gordon Cooper

21. In 1949 he landed the B-50 'Lucky Lady II' in Texas, completing the first around-the-world non-stop airplane flight. The flight lasted 94 hours and 1 minute and the plane was refueled four times in flight.

   A. Curtis LeMay   B. James Gallagher

   C. Jimmy Doolittle   D. Scott Crossfield

22. In 1962 he became the first U.S. astronaut in orbit – circling the earth three times before returning to earth.

   A. Walter Schirra, Jr.   B. Gordon Cooper

   C. Gus Grissom   D. John Glenn

23. In 1969 he became the first U.S. astronaut, and the first man to set foot on the moon.

   A. Neil Armstrong   B. Buzz Aldrin

   C. Michael Collins   D. Yuri Gagarin

24. In 1977 this American entreprenaur and co-founder of Apple helped usher in the era of the personal computer.

   A. Jeff Bezos   B. Charles Babbage

C. Steve Jobs   D. Konrad Zuse

25. In 1978, this Italian mountaineer and explorer made the first documented solo ascent of Mount Everest. He was the first to do so without contained oxygen for breathing, and was the first person to climb all 14 of the world's mountains that exceed an elevation of 26,250 ft.

A. Peter Habeler   B. Reinhold Messner

C. Edmund Hillary   D. George Mallory

Answers - Chapter 26 - Achievements Throughout History

1. A - John Jeffries

2. C - John Fitch

3. D - Samuel Hopkins

4. C - George Washington

5. B - Eli Whitney

6. A - Lewis & Clark

7. D - Noah Webster

8. C - Robert Fulton

9. B - Bonneville & Walker

10. C - P.T. Barnum

11. A - Samuel Morse

12. B - James Marshall

13. A - Olmsted & Vaux

14. D - John McDermott

15. C - Robert Peary

16. B - Eugene Ely

17. A - Ray Harroun

18. D - Charles Lindbergh

19. C - Gutzon Borglum

20. A - Chuck Yeager

21. B - James Gallagher

22. D – John Glenn

Did You Know: *In 1998 he became the oldest astronaut in space at the age of 77 when he returned to space.*

23. A – Neil Armstrong

24. C – Steve Jobs

25. B – Reinhold Messner

27

Men In Modern American History

Answers for this chapter on page 266

1. He was a legendary mountain man and fur trader whose expeditions during the height of the fur trade years were deemed as the most dangerous explorations. He was killed by Comanche Indians.

    A. Kit Carson   B. Jedediah Smith

    C. John "Grizzly" Adams   D. John Colter

2. He was one of the most powerful bankers of his time. He financed railroads, helped organize U.S. Steel, G.E., and other major corporations. He was also accused of manipulating the nation's financial system for his own gain.

    A. J.P. Morgan   B. Andrew Carnegie

    C. George Soros   D. Mayer Rothschild

3. He was an American ornithologist (person who studies birds), illustrator, and painter who for half a century was a wildlife artist. He is well-known for his drawings and paintings of North American birds.

A. Bill Oddie   B. Louis Fuertes

C. Paul Johnsgard   D. John James Audubon

4. He was a world leader of the Art Nouveau Movement; as revered for his exquisite jewelry as he was for his stained glass lamps and windows. He was an internationally renowned glass maker and was commissioned by President Chester Arthur to decorate the White House.

A. Marcel Wolfers   B. Louis Comfort Tiffany

C. Antonin Daum   D. Jacques Gruber

5. This Scottish-American, an advocate for the preservation of wilderness in the U.S. was known as "Father of the National Parks." He founded the Sierra Club and helped establish Sequoia and Yosemite National Parks in California.

A. Theodore Roosevelt B. Arthur Carhart

C. John Muir   D. Robert Marshall

6. These two brothers invented and flew the first powered and piloted airplane.

A. Lumière Brothers   B. Duryea Brothers

C. Wright Brothers   D. Merage Brothers

7. He was one of America's most notorious gangsters and became extremely wealthy during Prohibition bringing in $100 million a year by controlling illegal alcohol, prostitution, and gambling in Chicago.

A. Al Capone   B. Bugsy Siegel

C. Lucky Luciano   D. Sam Giancana

8. At the time of Prohibition this immigrant from the Rhineland was in the brewery business and became the first brewer to succeed at bottling beer for shipment. At the time of Prohibition he was the most powerful brewer of his day owning railroads, ice factories, and bottling plants. He built his family firm into the largest brewery in the western hemisphere.

    A. Adolph Coors   B. Adolphus Busch

    C. Frederick Pabst   D. David G. Yuengling

9. The Texas oil boom began Jan. 10Th, 1901 which was the most famous date in Texas oil. This mining engineer drilling at Spindletop, near Beaumont, had a great gusher erupt at the oil well he was drilling.

    A. Capt. A.F. Lucas   B. Colonel Edwin L. Drake

    C. Louis Evans   D. William Smith

10. This American industrialist amassed a fortune in the steel industry. He led the enormous expansion of the American steel industry, saw himself as a hero of working people, became a major philanthropist, and became one of the richest men in the world.

    A. DuPont   B. Carnegie

    C. Rockefeller   D. Astor

11. In 1903 the first World Series of MLB was played. It was the Boston Americans (Red Sox) against the Pittsburgh Pirates. Choose from the list below the star player who played in the first World Series, but never played in another World Series game.

    A. Cy Young   B. Honus Wagner

    C. Chick Stahl   D. Deacon Phillipe

12. All due to a $50 bet that he couldn't make it from San Francisco to

New York City in a "newfangled horseless carriage" in less than 90 days, he became the first person (along with his partner Sewall Crocker who was a bicycle racer and mechanic) to drive an automobile across the U.S.

    A. Wiley Post   B. George Wyman

    C. Thomas Stevens   D. Horatio Nelson Jackson

13. In 1906, which president signed into place the Antiquities Act; establishing archeological sites on public lands to be preserved for future generations.

    A. Theodore Roosevelt   B. Abraham Lincoln

    C. Franklin D. Roosevelt   D. Benjamin Harrison

14. He and his crew are credited with being the first men in history to reach the North Pole.

    A. Richard Byrd   B. Roald Amundsen

    C. Robert Peary   D. Matthew Henson

15. If you've visited the Smithsonian's Air and Space Museum in Washington, D.C. you may have discovered an exhibit honoring a man you may have never heard of. He was a pilot who made history by being the first man to not only land on but also take off of a ship.

    A. Edwin Dunning   B. Jake West

    C. James Flatley III   D. Eugene Ely

16. In 1911 he made the first transatlantic airplane flight across the United States.

    A. Charles Lindbergh   B. Wiley Post

C. C.P. Rogers   D. Chuck Downey

17. Born in Hungary, he and his family immigrated to the U.S. when he was still a child. He became one of the most famous and well-known magicians in history. He was the greatest escape artist of all time.

    A. Merlin   B. Harry Houdini

    C. David Copperfield   D. David Blaine

18. In 1913 the construction of the Panama Canal came to a close when which U.S. president began the explosion of the Gamboa Dike?

    A. Woodrow Wilson   B. Franklin D. Roosevelt

    C. Rutherford B. Hayes   D. Dwight D. Eisenhower

19. In 1925 this high school science teacher was prosecuted for teaching evolution in a Tennessee public school, hence what came to be known as "The Monkey Trial."

    A. Charles Darwin   B. John Scopes

    C. Charles Lyell   D. James Hutton

20. He is the most famous aviator in history, having earned that by being the first to complete a nonstop transatlantic flight from New York to Paris in his plane called, 'The Spirit of St. Louis.'

    A. Orville Wright   B. Robert Hoover

    C. Eddie Rickenbacker   D. Charles Lindbergh

21. This American sculptor is best known as the sculptor of Mount Rushmore.

A. Robert Glenn   B. Edward Eriksen

C. Gutzon Borglum   D. Frederic Auguste Bartholdi

22. He is the astronomer who discovered Pluto.

A. Johann Gottfried Galle   B. Clyde Tombaugh

C. Nicolaus Copernicus   D. Edmond Halley

23. He is one of the most famous federal agents in the history of law enforcement after pulling off the extraordinary, something no one thought could be done. He was the Prohibition agent who gained fame for leading a group of "untouchable" federal agents who raided Al Capone's breweries in Chicago which broke the back of organized crime in Chicago.

A. Chester Gould   B. Harry Elliott

C. Levi Trexler   D. Eliot Ness

24. He was an American landscape photographer whose black and white photographic images of America's West are easily recognizable as his work.

A. Ansel Adams   B. Edward Weston

C. Darren white   D. Charlie Waite

25. He is America's most famou architect. He designed structures in harmony with their environment. One of his designs, *Falling Water* is one of the most unique houses in the world.

A. Richard Morris Hunt   B. Frank Lloyd Wright

C. Frank Gehry   D. I.M. Pei

26. Perhaps the first world-wide "fake news" broadcast was by this man over the radio on Halloween night in 1938. He gave a dramatization of an alien invasion on earth titled 'War of the Worlds' causing a nation wide panic with people believing a Martian invasion was taking place on Earth.

    A. Peter Ustinov   B. Del Moore

    C. Orson Welles   D. Graham McNamee

27. This German born physicist influenced the beginning of the Manhattan Project.

    A. Albert Einstein   B. Harold Urey

    C. Enrico Fermi   D. Edward Teller

28. He was a German engineer who played a prominent role in rocketry and space exploration, first in Germany and after WWII in the U.S. At the end of WWII he and the entire German rocket development team surrendered to U.S. troops and within a few months were working at White Sands, New Mexico working on all aspects of rockets and guided missiles. He was later on the team that launched the first U.S. satellite.

    A. Edward Teller   B. Klaus Fuchs

    C. Niels Bohr   D. Wernher von Braun

29. He was an Air Force test pilot who was the first person to break the sound barrier.

    A. John Glenn   B. Sam Shepard

    C. Chuck Yeager   D. Bud Anderson

30. He was the most visible face and outcry during the Cold War. He tried to expose the communists and those who were considered risks to

the U.S.

A. J. Edgar Hoover B. Joseph McCarthy

C. Roy Cohn D. Alger Hiss

31. It is said his idea to create his famous theme park came to him while taking his daughters for a ride on a merry-go-round. He was an animator, voice actor, and film producer who along with his brother opened the most famous theme parks in the world.

A. Carl Laemmie B. George Millay

C. Walt Disney D. Angus Wynne

32. In 1961 he became the first American to travel in space and in 1971 he walked on the moon.

A. Alan Shepard B. John Glenn

C. Neil Armstrong D. Gus Grissom

33. On November 22, 1963 while riding in a presidential motorcade in Dallas, Texas what president was assassinated?

A. Abraham Lincoln B. William McKinley

C. John F. Kennedy D. James Garfield

34. He was accused of assassinating President John F. Kennedy.

A. Leon Czolgosz B. John Wilkes Booth

C. John Hinckley Jr. D. Lee Harvey Oswald

35. Two days after being accused and arrested of assassinating President Kennedy he was shot to death in the basement of the Dallas police station by this man, a nightclub owner with connections to organized crime.

    A. James Earl Ray   B. Jack Ruby

    C. Sirhan Sirhan   D. J. D. Tippit

36. He was the parent of a student who filed the lawsuit in Abingdon School District that legally mandated Bible reading or prayer in public schools as unconstitutional. It was due to this man that the landmark Supreme Court decision kicked God and prayer out of the schools.

    A. Edward Schempp   B. Vashti McCollum

    C. Jack Phillips   D. David Josiah Brewer

37. This Civil Rights leader who led with nonviolent protests was shot and killed by a sniper as he stood on the balcony of his motel room killing him at the age of 39.

    A. Mahatma Gandhi   B. Nelson Mandela

    C. Malcolm X   D. Martin Luther King, Jr.

38. He was the first African-American Justice of the Supreme Court.

    A. Clarence Thomas   B. Byron White

    C. William Rehnquist   D. Thurgood Marshall

39. He murdered Martin Luther King, Jr. and eluded the police for two months.

    A. Mark David Chapman   B. James Earl Ray

C. Jared Loughner   D. James Holmes

40. He was the brother of a president who also had his eyes on the presidency for himself. Previously a U.S. Attorney and a senator he fought organized crime and worked for civil rights. While campaigning for the presidency he was shot and died the following day.

   A. Billy Carter   B. Neil Bush

   C. Robert Kennedy   D. Roger Clinton

41. He was convicted of fatally shooting Robert Kennedy in 1968.

   A. Sirhan Sirhan   B. Richard Pavlick

   C. Richard Lawrence   D. John Schrank

42. *American Top 40*, hosted by what radio personality became the first successful nationally syndicated radio program featuring a weekly countdown.

   A. Wolfman Jack   B. Casey Kasem

   C. Dick Clark   D. Don Cornelius

43. He is the billionaire co-founder of Microsoft.

   A. Steve Wozniak   B. Bill Gates

   C. Larry Page   D. Jeff Bezos

44. He was the U.S. Airways pilot when two minutes into the flight a flock of birds flew into both engines and he ditched the plane with 155 people aboard into the Hudson River saving all lives becoming an American hero.

A. Abbie Hoffman   B. "Sully" Chesley Sullenberger

C. Dalton Trumbo   D. William Kyle Carpenter

45. He is the founder of SpaceX and co-founder of Tesla. He sent a rocket into space launching a Tesla car into orbit around Mars in 2018.

A. Elon Musk   B. Steve Jobs

C. Mark Zuckerberg   D. Jeff Bezos

Answers - Chapter 27 – Men In Modern American History

1. B – Jedediah Smith

2. A – J.P. Morgan

3. D – John James Audubon

4. B – Louis Comfort Tiffany

5. C – John Muir

6. C – Wright Brothers

Did You Know: While growing up in the Wright home the children were encouraged to pursue intellectual interests and whatever aroused their curiosity. Wilbur and Orville were the only children in the family who did not attend college. The brothers enjoyed watching birds and observed the birds as they were in flight, as the air flowed over their wings causing lift, and they noticed the birds changed the shape of their wings when turning. They used this information when designing their plane. Their father, a minister of the church who had encouraged their pursuits in the past differed when it came to their building a "flying machine." He considered it blasphemy and told them it would be impossible for men to fly in the future.

7. A – Al Capone

8. B – Adolphus Busch

9. A – Capt. A. F. Lucas

10. B – Carnegie

11. A – Cy Young

12. D – Horatio Nelson Jackson

13. A – Theodore Roosevelt

14. C – Robert Peary

15. D – Eugene Ely

16. C – C.P. Rodgers

Did You Know: William Randolph Hearst offered a $50,000 prize for the first person who could fly from coast to coast in less than 30 days. Rodger's only had 90 minutes of flight instruction from Orville Wright before he made his first solo flight. He flew out of New York with the final destination being Pasadena, California. He made it after more than 15 crash landings, but he missed the deadline by 19 days.

17. B – Harry Houdini

18. A – Woodrow Wilson

19. B – John Scopes

20. D – Charles Lindbergh

Did You Know: Lindbergh was a hero with clay feet. He was the darling of America when he made his historic flight and the world mourned with him when in 1932 his 20 month old son was kidnapped from his crib and found dead. But attitudes toward this hero changed when in 1936 he was invited by high-ranking Nazi official Hermann Göring to tour their aircraft facilities and when in 1938 he received the German Service Cross from Göring. The previously adoring American public were outraged by his seemingly Nazi connections and the fact that he was rubbing shoulders with the enemy. A speech he gave was widely criticized as anti-Semitic and racist, views the Nazis themselves held. Appartently that wasn't all that he was doing in Germany. It was discovered after his death that he was a serial adulterer. He had 5 more children with his wife after the death of their firstborn, but he also had 7 other children by 3 different German women – all confirmed by DNA testing. As one of his illegitimate children, Astrid Bouteuil said, "The fact that we exist testifies to the fact that he was simply a man – not a hero."

21. C – Gutzon Borglum

Did You Know: He was famous before sculpting the president's heads at Mount Rushmore. Some of his art was displayed in Windsor Castle, he was a gold medal winner at the 1904 St. Louis Exposition, and a bust of President Lincoln displayed in the White House (currently in the Rotunda at the Capitol) were some of his works. The four presidents carved at Mount Rushmore were chosen as Borglum thought they represented the most important events in U.S. history. Washington was chosen for leading the colonists in the Revolutionary War, for being the "Father of the Country", and for laying the foundation of American democracy. Thomas Jefferson was chosen as the primary author of the Declaration of Independence and for doubling the size of the country through the Louisiana Purchase. Theodore Roosevelt linked the east with the Panama Canal. Abraham Lincoln held the nation together preserving the union.

22. B – Clyde Tombaugh

23. D – Eliot Ness

24. A – Ansel Adams

25. B – Frank Lloyd Wright

26. C – Orson Welles

27. A – Albert Einstein

Did You Know: the Manhattan Project was the undertaking of scientists and military developing the atomic bomb.

28. D – Wernher von Braun

29. C – Chuck Yeager

30. B – Joseph McCarthy

31. C – Walt Disney

32. A – Alan Shepard

33. C – John F. Kennedy

34. D – Lee Harvey Oswald

35. B – Jack Ruby

36. A – Edward Schempp

37. D – Martin Luther King, Jr.

38. D – Thurgood Marshall

39. B – James Earl Ray

40. C – Robert Kennedy

41. A – Sirhan Sirhan

Did You Know: The Kennedy family is a family rife with conspiracy theories. In *this case, even the son of Robert Kennedy says he's not convinced that Sirhan Sirhan killed his father, believing a 2nd shooter was involved. Kennedy Jr. went so far as to meet with Sirhan Sirhan, the man charged with killing his father for 3 hours, reviewed autopsy reports, police reports, and interviewed witnesses. The evidence just didn't add up – at least as far as Sirhan Sirhan being the only shooter. Paul Schrade, the man directly behind Robert Kennedy at the time he was shot who was also shot gave compelling evidence as to the reasoning behind the allegations of a 2nd shooter. It isn't only Robert Kennedy's son, but lawyers of Sirhan Sirhan who claim he was a Manchurian candidate who was hypnotized and was not acting under his own volition, but hypno-programmed into carrying out a violent act. Many have pointed their fingers at the CIA, the same as they did with Robert Kennedy's brother the president's assassination. They believe the CIA had a hand in both of their deaths.*

42. B – Casey Kasem

43. B – Bill Gates

44. B - "Sully" Chesley Sullenberger

45. A – Elon Musk

A message to my readers:

I hope you enjoyed testing your memory and having fun with this trivia / history book. I'm sure you have thought of other great names that weren't included in the book. There just comes a point when you have to stop somewhere and hope you can include the other names in another book in the future.

Thank you for purchasing my book. If you enjoyed it please do take the time to leave feedback . You may also want to check out my book 'Women In History Trivia.'

Cheryl Pryor

www.ingramcontent.com/pod-product-compliance
Lightning Source LLC
Chambersburg PA
CBHW060500090426
42735CB00011B/2050